The HOPE *for* AUDACITY

CRITICAL EDUCATION & ETHICS

Barry Kanpol
General Editor

Vol. 3

The Critical Education and Ethics series
is part of the Peter Lang Education list.
Every volume is peer reviewed and meets
the highest quality standards for content and production.

PETER LANG
New York • Washington, D.C./Baltimore • Bern
Frankfurt • Berlin • Brussels • Vienna • Oxford

The HOPE *for* AUDACITY

From Cynicism *to* Hope *in* Educational Leadership *and* Policy

Edited by
Stella C. Batagiannis, Barry Kanpol,
and Anna V. Wilson

PETER LANG
New York • Washington, D.C./Baltimore • Bern
Frankfurt • Berlin • Brussels • Vienna • Oxford

Library of Congress Cataloging-in-Publication Data

The hope for audacity: from cynicism to hope in educational leadership and policy / edited by Stella C. Batagiannis, Barry Kanpol, Anna V. Wilson.
pages cm. — (Critical education and ethics; vol. 3)
Includes bibliographical references and index.
1. Educational change—United States. 2. Education and state—United States.
3. Public schools—United States.
I. Batagiannis, Stella C. II. Kanpol, Barry. III. Wilson, Anna Victoria.
IV. Title: From cynicism to hope in educational leadership and policy.
LA217.2H65 371.2—dc23 2012008475
ISBN 978-1-4331-1859-3 (hardcover)
ISBN 978-1-4331-1858-6 (paperback)
ISBN 978-1-4539-0803-7 (e-book)
ISSN 2166-1359

Bibliographic information published by **Die Deutsche Nationalbibliothek**.
Die Deutsche Nationalbibliothek lists this publication in the "Deutsche Nationalbibliografie"; detailed bibliographic data is available on the Internet at http://dnb.d-nb.de/.

The paper in this book meets the guidelines for permanence and durability of the Committee on Production Guidelines for Book Longevity of the Council of Library Resources.

29 Broadway, 18th floor, New York, NY 10006
www.peterlang.com

Printed in the United States of America

Dedication

This book is dedicated to educational leaders, teachers, and the children they serve—to offer hope as these educators struggle against the ideological grain of privatization and market logic.

Contents

Part Three: Democracy as the Foundation of Policy

Acknowledgments

Heartfelt thanks to Barry Kanpol, Series Editor and Co-editor of this book, whose visionary leadership inspired the trilogy and who has caused all of us to think deeply about the political climate challenging education today—and how to lead beyond the resulting limits.

Special Thanks

Special thanks to Dawn Adams, our administrative assistant, who has been invaluable in addressing all of the critical details of formatting a book for publication—and always with patience and enthusiasm.

Introduction

Kenneth Tye

Good Intentions

In July 2010, President Barack Obama spoke about education reform at the National Urban League Centennial Conference. Much of what he had to say was welcomed by the education community. For example, he spoke forcefully about the need to strengthen early childhood education, higher education, and, in particular, the education of students who come from disadvantaged backgrounds. He also spent a good deal of time on the idea that we need to do all we can to support the teaching force in our schools. It is interesting to note that these are ideas that have been with us for a long time and were clearly set forth in the creation of Head Start, Job Corps, and the Community Action Programs of the Office of Economic Opportunity (OEO) Program established in 1964, as well as the Elementary and Secondary Education Act (ESEA) of 1965. It seemed that a president would finally fulfill old promises!

The Disconnect between Intentions and Actions

The problem, of course, is the gap between good intentions and thoughtful action. Most Americans, and particularly the education community, have strongly supported the president because of his statements about his intentions with regard to our schools. Barry Kanpol, the author of Chapter 1 in this book, points out that President Obama has suggested that *The Audacity of Hope* is a call to educational action for the nation. However, as Kanpol also notes, many of us have interpreted this to mean a Hope for Audacity or, in other words, a hope for bold, new actions.

In fact, the actions that have since been taken by President Obama are major disappointments. In his Urban League presentation, the president stated clearly that he believes that anyone who opposes his ideas for action is afraid of change. Yet he is the one who supports the tired old ideas of George

Bush's No Child Left Behind (NCLB) Act, signed into law in 2002 and based on market theory that arose from *A Nation at Risk* during President Ronald Reagan's administration in 1983. Clearly, critique is in order, and the authors in this book engage in thoughtful conversation about these very issues.

In Chapter 3, Jonathan Hilpert describes *A Nation at Risk* as a made-up "narrative about an educational system in crisis" that, in the years since 1983, has been used to promote its privatization. Further, Hilpert argues, it has promoted a sense of fear about the system and has detracted from truly critical thinking about the role public education plays in the lives of American children in a democratic society. In fact, the proponents of a market orientation, according to Hilpert, decry what they call the current "democratic control" of our schools because it stands in the way of further privatization of our educational system, a far cry from the deliberative democracy that Kathleen Murphey so eloquently argues for in Chapter 2.

Perhaps this deliberative democracy is closely linked in Chapter 7 by Jane Grant. Here Grant asserts that since the so-called Gingrich revolution in the 1990s, the radical right in this country has called for the privatization of a number of institutions that have "previously been accepted parts of the public sector: Social Security, public education, prisons and highway systems, and even defense and military functions" (p. 147). Additionally, market-based ideas in public education include the promotion of school vouchers, school choice, merit pay, performance incentives (and punishments), "contracting out" services, and business-operated schools, including privately run charter schools. It is these ideas, not at all new, that President Obama wants us to accept without question. It could well be argued that he is the one who is "afraid of change." One cannot help but ask: Where is the audacity of hope to change the ideology of Race to the Top dollars that Murphey considers?

While the answers to these questions are being sought, it becomes necessary to separate President Obama's rhetoric from his actions. Five of our authors address this issue in different ways. In Chapter 5, Marisol Rexach and Tom Wilson present a thorough dissection of Obama's speeches, which they say leads to some misgivings about Obama's educational rhetoric. The authors identify a "disconnect between his beliefs about social, forward-looking democratic change, and his support for what many perceived to be a regressive educational discourse characterized as unmitigated faith in technology, high-stakes testing, national and state standards, and—probably most significant—competitive economic efficacy" (p. 91). In addition, in Chapter 4, Stella Batagiannis demonstrates that Obama's actions do not differ significantly from those of conservatives who have attempted for the last 30 years to undermine public education with market-driven rationalities. Batagiannis argues that Obama has dashed educators' hopes of changing NCLB and its negative effects on learning and has promoted the ultra-competitive Race to the Top dollars linked to public schools. Batagiannis clearly says, "Obama's current actions belie very different dispositions from those his rhetoric led us to expect" (p. 72). As well, Kanpol and Grant in their chapters and Brian Fife in Chapter 6 echo analogous views.

Rexach and Wilson's critique of NCLB includes the inconsistent standards established independently by each state. As a result, in June 2010, a set of "Common Core Standards" for math and language arts was developed by the National Governors' Association in collaboration with the Council of Chief State School Officers (CCSSO). By the end of the summer, well over half of the states had adopted them. This is happening despite the fact pointed out by Hilpert that "experts in education and psychological measurement are in virtually unanimous agreement that most state-mandated tests are poor measurement instruments that fail to capture growth, especially in low-income schools" (p. 43).

In agreeing with the prior arguments, Hilpert supports the premise that all children deserve a quality education and that none "should be left behind," as Murphey maintains; otherwise we replicate or reproduce class and race inequities. Clearly, these authors argue that NCLB is flawed in many ways. The assessment requirements and the accountability (Fife) provisions attached to them are rigid and ultimately unworkable. They promote bad educational practices: teaching to the test, devaluation of subjects such as the social studies and the arts, lack of diagnosis of individual student needs, and lack of assessment of high-order thinking skills. Finally, Batagiannis, in a most important critique of NCLB, the title of which she terms "a powerful euphemism," points to its lack of authenticity, citing Jonathan Kozol (2005), who critiqued it as "basically driven by the concept that teachers have an inherently perverse attraction to mediocrity...and only if [threatened] will...aspire to excellence" (p. 64).

As a result of NCLB and advocates of high-stakes testing and market ideas, the assumption is that schools are beyond repair. Hilpert, however, states that there is much evidence to the contrary. Citing J. R. Flynn (1994) and Gerald Bracey (2003), he argues that both IQ and standardized test scores "have been on the rise for decades," as have problem-solving abilities, and "middle- and upper-class students in our country score in the top three on internationally norm-referenced math, science, and reading tests" (p. 42). Looking at it another way, Rexach and Wilson present evidence that American students in well-funded schools who come from high-income families outscore all or nearly all other countries on international tests. However, children in high-poverty schools score below the international average. Rexach and Wilson unequivocally state that our educational system has been successful. The problem is poverty, and the economic gap demonstrates our values. As Murphey hints, we value those who have, and we care little about the have-nots. Thus, according to Hilpert, what is happening is that policymakers, not wanting to tackle social ills such as poverty and deteriorating communities, shift the blame away from themselves and toward teachers and schools. The reality is that education is less part of the problem than it is part of the solution, but only a part.

Clearly, a neoliberal, market logic-led ideology has been front and center to the Obama administration. An early hint that Obama had been captured by market ideology was his appointment of Arne Duncan as Secretary of Education. This meant that there would be no audacious approach to the problems of American education. Rather, it meant that—as Kanpol concludes—Obama embraces the old ideas of the Bush administration, including seeking reform through high-stakes testing, increasing the militarization of public schools, and decreasing parent and community control of education.

Batagiannis concludes that Duncan is a politician, not an educator. As such, he has bought into the market view of how education should be reformed. In fact, Margaret Spellings, Secretary of Education under President George W. Bush, praised Duncan as a "fellow reformer." Prior to his federal appointment, he was superintendent of the Chicago public school system, and, as Batagiannis points out, he was less than a success in that job. She cites Diane Ravitch's (2010) criticism: "Chicago continues to be one of the lowest performing cities in the nation on the NAEP [National Assessment of Educational Progress]" (p. 79). Serious questions have been raised about Obama's selection of Duncan over authentic school reformers.

Duncan and Obama have developed what I discussed earlier as a Race to the Top plan. In Chapter 8, Penny Bryan describes the plan this way:

> Quietly, $4.3 billion of our tax money has been put in a pot with a small opening, fostering an economic model not constrained by the social and moral principles of liberty and justice for all. It is a public/private funding distribution based on a competitive model for states with a few winners making it to the top and all the remainder losers, which means that most of our students lose as well. It promotes funding with a standardized delivery that necessitates conformity to a one-size-fits-all definition of learning, entrance by lotteries, and success defined as high test scores. (p. 169).

On to the broader context now.

The Broader Context

Thus far, what has been presented is a critique of President Obama's actions directed at improving American education. Moving beyond critique, it is important to note that a major strength of this book is that the discussion is set within a broader societal context. Further, it is also critical to note that without such a consideration of context, there will continue to be an endless string of "quick fixes" proposed for our schools rather than a thoughtful and thorough look at problems and possible solutions.

Bryan begins her chapter by setting Obama's intentions within a framework of ideal principles of democracy. She points out that such principles were fully explained in John Dewey's *Democracy and Education* in 1916: "In failing to recognize the necessity of democracy for education, the mission of our schools has become more focused on narrowly conceived 'results'" (p. 164). "Renewal in education…means creating more democratic schools in which the freedom to make choices and take action teaches each student the responsibility for his or her own learning" (p. 165). This is in contrast to the view that participatory democracy is unworkable and that governance should be delegated exclusively to political representatives and their expert advisors.

And Bryan delves more deeply into the ideas of Dewey and other scholars concerned with the relationship between education and democracy. She examines the history of democracy in an effort to seek out answers to the current problems of education, and she then looks at where public education seems to be headed in the Obama administration, toward the strengthening of the concepts and responsibilities of democratic beliefs. Bryan would agree with Murphey that alliances of consent are needed to push education away from market-led operations.

Clearly, Fife would agree that if Obama would embrace the notion that democratic deliberation can yield positive and tangible policy results, a far more educated citizenry would be the result. Although these ideas are not new, Fife does a fine job of documenting their history. He also states that "Democracy is not a passive entity by definition." He goes on to say that "The Educated citizens are inclined to acquire civic values and a sense of common national identity" (p. 126). A major historical proposition of this process is that the common school experience is important to the development of such a democracy. Further, Fife concludes, "The assault on the common school ideology with regard to the choice, privatization, and even charter schools [is having] a harmful consequence" (pp. 128–129) with regard to our search for a truly democratic society. If there is to be accountability, it falls to the federal government and its leaders to see that this assault does not succeed.

To succeed, however, Grant would argue that a new social contract, a common good, clearly sets forth agreed-upon civic rights as well as obligations. Such obligations could include what we owe to others in our country, to future generations, to other nations, and to other species. The proposed way to identify such rights and obligations is through public deliberations that require citizens to reason with each other, and it takes place in public spaces within a deliberative democracy.

Personal Identification with Obama and Disappointment

Many Obama supporters were taken with his clear rhetoric, precision, and personality. Thus, Batagiannis and Kanpol bring to the discussion a different kind of contextual variable: their own life experiences. That is, thcy tell how they identify with Obama because of the similarity of their family histories and their own leadership roles. They explain how such identification caused them to relate to the president and his rhetoric. Unfortunately, like many of his early education supporters, they began to lose their identification with him because his actions did not match his rhetoric. This disconnect between words and actions is a huge disappointment to a great number of those who have spent much of their careers working to improve our schools, and it is a major theme of this book. It also makes me ask whether Obama's early rhetoric was truly authentic.

The Future

Formulating a critique is relatively easy to do. Facilitating a solution is a bit more difficult. In the end, what is most important, though more difficult, is the thoughtful setting forth of suggestions for correcting the problems identified in the critique. Simply stated, the question is: Where do we go from here?

As of this writing, most conscientious and thoughtful educators and community members support the notion that public schools should be dedicated to the public good and that they should not be randomly driven to respond to market ideas. Unfortunately they observe that, in contrast to his stated belief in democratic ideals for the schools, Obama supports market ideas. His actions simply have not matched his rhetoric.

At the macro level, people of good will should begin to think of the term that Arne Duncan likes to use: *accountability*. Unfortunately for him, that has come to mean that the schools are failing, and teachers and administrators therefore need to be punished. The fact is that Obama and Duncan must be held accountable. In terms of Duncan, we should perhaps begin the process of seeking a replacement for him. He is simply not qualified for the job, and he leads the movement to destroy public education. Obama will be held accountable in 2012 when people go to the polls to express their beliefs about what he has or has not accomplished during his term as president. People who believe in the importance of public education as a vehicle for promoting the common good and democratic goals in our society will have the chance to register their displeasure with his educational actions or lack thereof.

Obama can avoid finding himself turned out of office by some of the people who were originally among his most ardent supporters because of his expressed beliefs and his own personal history. To begin with, he could acknowledge his mistakes and admit that he has not followed his stated agenda. He can either work to get rid of NCLB and Race to the Top, or at least propose significant changes in both having to do with promoting democracy and the common good rather than market ideas.

Batagiannis argues that a disconnect between rhetoric and action is evidence of inauthentic behavior, which can lead us to "increasing privatization; growing commitment to individualism; worshiping of the market, continuing to allow obscene amounts of wealth to be amassed by a few at the expense of the broader American society" (p. 82); and increasing control over public education by policy makers who seem to have little real knowledge of what it takes to develop high-quality education.

Also, Batagiannis points out that if Obama wishes to change course and lead us down a "road of authenticity, that road will be one of a democratic community in which we value and respect each other as human beings" (p. 82). Furthermore, "Education, not schooling, will be the emphasis....Educators will be respected for their work, not blamed for social ills beyond their control...educators and policy makers will join hands to meet today's new challenges, focusing on the overarching goal of teaching children to love learning, to problem solve, to think deeply and critically, and to be good citizens" (p. 82) rather than learn to fill in the bubbles on tests, which
reflects rote memorization instead of critical thinking.

Rather than making pronouncements about simplistic and harmful market ideas, what is needed right now, according to Kanpol, is "to open up spaces [at every level] for [inclusive] dialogue and critical thought," or a deliberative democracy. Such dialogue requires that schools and policy makers need to reach out to community members about community quality of life issues, including, but not limited to, educational issues. Rexach and Wilson make it clear that simply talking is not enough. Both conservatives and liberals tend to use words such as *democracy*, and it is important that people explore the meaning of such words, as well as come to agreement about such meanings. With this in mind, Bryan points out, quoting Deborah Meier (2003): "The importance of face to face encounters between people with differing views and the related capacity to imagine a viewpoint different from one's own are intellectual habits of mind" (p. 177) and central to an active democracy. She cites Henry Giroux (2009): "We do need some new language to define the meaning and purpose of public and higher education, one that makes democracy [with public involvement] its defining principle....This is a view of education that treats teachers as critical and supportive intellectuals, students as engaged citizens, not consumers, and schools as democratic public spheres, not training sites for the business world" (p. 178). In other words, new social movements and accountable and principled leaders are important to what Grant calls "a new social compact." Here we must "discuss our values...[and be able to state them so] that others can understand and even accept" [them].

In summary, democratic deliberation speaks to public issues, and it takes place in public spaces. Such deliberation should be able to reduce some of the concerns we have that we have lost the ability to discuss political issues within an ethical or value-oriented framework.

On a more practical level, Bryan sets forth a statement of hope for new realities that strengthens democracy and education. This statement includes suggestions such as: (1) stop schooling our children as if they were products and reclaim our schools as sacred places for human beings; and (2) rethink our classrooms as vibrant spaces that awaken consciousness to the world, open minds to the problems of the human condition, inspire wonder, and help people to lead personally fulfilling lives. If our democracy is to thrive, our schools must change into these exciting spaces. Otherwise, we will not be a democracy "of the people," but rather a corporate nation of workers, TV viewers, and shoppers.

To develop this important statement, Bryan points to the work of several people who have described how a democracy requires opportunities and experiences that develop the whole child with open, serious habits of mind, heart, and art (for example, John Dewey, Paulo Freire, Elliot Eisner, Maxine Greene, Deborah Meier, Nel Noddings, and Alfie Kohn). Such habits are best formed when there is a "seamless integration of meaning and real life [with] connections in and out of school [where] authentic and enduring education can take place" (p. 176). She goes on with this line of thinking by pointing out that when "politics and policies that are vastly different from No Child Left Behind support intellectual and humane architecture and civic engagement, then such a society can hope and act for a better future" (p. 176). In conclusion, Bryan identifies and describes numerous organizations across the country that support the development of public democratic schools. Similarly, Kanpol, in describing how schools and colleges of education might develop democratic programs that prepare teachers and other educators, proposes a new vision of field placements—ones that are not simply technical assignments but are connected to service learning in the community in which one is placed.

Linking Practice and Theories of Educational Change

In many ways, the authors of this volume have offered personal, theoretical, and practical insights into Obama's relationship to education. Although the "hope" has not been lost, it has certainly come under question. It seems that theoretical constructs such as systems theory, transformational leadership, formative evaluation, linkage to knowledge, reflection, stages of change, group decision making and problem solving, and school culture need to further develop the well-crafted arguments in this book so that "hope" can really be audacious. Thus, it is fair to say that the book and its argument are still a work in progress. Perhaps, as the authors have articulated, some serious dialogue needs to take place among policy makers, educational leaders, and community members at all levels of society. Such a dialogue can bring new hope for schools. It can allow the rebirth of hope in "Yes we can!"

References

Bracey, G. (2003). Those misleading SAT and NAEP trends: Simpson's paradox at work. Education Disinformation Detection and Reporting Agency. Retrieved May 2010 from http://www.america-tomorrow./bracey/EDDRA/EDDRA30.htm\

Dewey, J. (1916). *Democracy and education*. New York: Macmillan. Quoted from W.H. Garrison. (March 2003). Democracy, experience, and education: Promoting a continued capacity for growth. *Phi Delta Kappan, 87*(7), 525–529.

Flynn, J.R. (1994). IQ gains over time. In R.J. Sternberg (Ed.), *Encyclopedia of human intelligence* (pp. 617–623). New York: Macmillan.

Giroux, A. (2009). Obama's view of education is stuck in reverse. Retrieved February 2010 from www.truth.org

Ravitch, D. (2010). *The death and life of the great American school system*. New York: Basic Books.

❖ PART ONE ❖

TOGETHER WE CAN

❖ CHAPTER ONE ❖

True to Self and the Institutionalization of a New Public Identity: It's Not Only Up to Barack Obama!

Barry Kanpol

Like many Americans whom I both know and don't know, the election of Barack Obama to the presidency injected an energy into politics and everyday experiences that was matched by little else in the history of this great country. Personally, I bought into the popular view or what Grossberg (1992) has labeled "affective investments." Here, collective and personal experience is reduced to the hype, hope, hyperbole, and expectation of the dominant views that—quite simply put—because we have now elected a president of color, and no less an intellectual, the historical order of the way business is done in education will change. The hope was that, in part, we were obtaining leadership that was able to see through the contradictions of a system that claimed democratic virtue in the face of a competitive market logic, which purported a community logic while reeking of rampant individualism and professed diversity of experience as paramount while promoting a one-size-fits-all mentality.

Reading Obama's two main books, *Dreams from My Father* and *The Audacity of Hope*, I was struck by his intellectual fluidity—his ability to transfer intellectual argument to paper. Perhaps more important, I emotionally responded to Obama's personal family history. Quite simply, it influenced me. I also come from parents from different countries—a father who was born in China from Russian parents and a mother who was born in Poland whose whole family vanished in the Holocaust. Now in the United States, with this history in mind, a president elect promised an allegiance to an alternative politics, even immersed himself in difference and nonconformity to the status quo. I resonated. I admired. I lost myself in my history and connected that with the history of the president elect. I am quite sure that I was not the only one who did this in diverse American communities!

Apart from immigrant commonalities to Obama, as dean of a College of Education and Public Policy with many years of leadership behind me, I also understood that while leadership looks different to different folk in various institutional hierarchies, we too had some common threads here. Whether it be politicking for position, dealing with institutionalized standards, or making tough calls, talking about leadership and doing it are two different animals. This is why in an article I wrote entitled "Critical Educational Leadership: Put Up or Shut Up!" (2002), I called into question how leaders (in my case, educational leaders in higher education) constantly struggle to walk the talk of social justice in the face of institutional barriers.[1] Talking about "social justice" and doing it, so to speak, often find roads that do not merge. What I have realized over the years in my own leadership style, or even philosophy, is that oftentimes one's history, personal commitments, and philosophies can be compromised in the face of institutional hegemonies, such as a consumer market logic philosophy. After reading about Barack Obama's history and the attending critiques of his educational philosophies and practices by many academics, I am convinced that as educational leaders we all resonate with some of Obama's history as a leader—personal commitment in the face of harsh institutional realities. However, as leaders know, we can aid personal philosophy with choice of other leaders, the ability to challenge instantaneous perfection or a quick fix with the courage to challenge it (Batagiannis 2007), or, quite simply, walking the grey lines of the personal desires versus institutional hegemony to affect change in a broad way, one connected to our field in education.

Most critiques I have read of Obama's educational philosophies and practices remain in the cynical mode: critique for the sake of critique, or bashing for the sake of bashing. Yes, I have played that game before—well over 20 years now, ever since I graduated with my doctorate. It is easy to critique as a way out of dealing with authentic change efforts. To be sure, it is less easy to offer hope out of despair, or possibility out of cynicism, and view a glass that is half full rather than half empty. With the above in mind, this chapter will (a) pit semblances of Obama's and my own personal link of self and history to educational philosophy, (b) view the contradiction of democratic hope in the face of institutional educational constraints, and (c) outline what I believe is a response to the conundrums I will deal with by discussing the importance of what I will describe as a renewed public identity in the face of "corporate" hegemony. Finally, I will reflect on my own leadership and link it instructively with the hope that perhaps one day this chapter and others on Barack Obama can be read by those in institutional spheres of influence.

Self and Educational Philosophy: Historical Oppression versus Growing Up with Privilege

Although I do not want to reduce one's self and experience to ultimate truth, it goes without saying that the historical construction of what Sharon Welch (1990) described as the "recollection of dangerous memories" can color how one views the world and ultimately help establish philosophical viewpoints. To be able to understand one's own place in the world in relation to the structure in which one has lived, as well as to challenge various forms of oppression, subordination, and alienation, Welch argued that one would have to first recollect one's own personal forms of oppression to be able to put oneself into the shoes of another's oppression—or at least understand it as well as possible. With that knowledge gained, then, one would have the ability to plan to change oppressed experiences and/or structures.

This is not the place to delve into every personal fact of the president's life that has been made public. His book *Dreams from My Father: A Story of Race and Inheritance* allows us many glimpses of Obama's complicated history and the construction of his historical beliefs. Certainly, we learn of the collection of his dangerous memories, the countries he lived in, and the school systems he attended. Although Obama's grandparents had been hailed as both "Nigger lovers" and "dirty Yankees," they instilled a solid work ethic into his consciousness. My grandparents on my mother's side were obliterated by anti-Semitic hate. As late as the early 1970s, I, too, would face the "dirty Jew" sing-song by too many folk to count in Melbourne, Australia. Perhaps I resonate with Obama in some important aspects, for instance, youthful exuberance and the willingness to suspend belief that discrimination was overt, like Obama, whose "father looked nothing like the people around me—that he was black as pitch, my mother white as milk—barely registered in my mind." Although my grandparents spoke only Yiddish in Australia or broken English at best, I loved their commitment to maintaining their culture through their language and ethnic food, as well as their sheer survival instincts as evidenced by their leaving Poland in a timely fashion and their struggle to make ends meet in Australia—all in my mind to give their offspring a better life than they had experienced in war-torn Europe. What I didn't understand or register as a child growing up was the historical pain they must have felt at the discrimination they had experienced through the Hitler regime. The smiles on their faces at the traditional Passover dinners masked the dangerous memories constructed in their lives, as well as their past oppressive and shattering experiences.

I don't want to assume that the president's relationship to historical oppression through race and/or mixed marriage of his white mother or black father and Indonesian stepfather—or that my own memories depicted above are similar. They are clearly different. Yet the commonality of dangerous memory has been handed down and publicly written about by both Obama (2006) and myself (1999). On a personal level, I grew to understand about social injustices by experiencing them in the post-Holocaust era, in Australia through discrimination of Jewish boys (Kanpol, 1999). Obama, it seems, grew to appreciate the mixture of cultures in his own history while being aware of aspects of the historical discrimination of that particular history. Given his history, he comments profoundly on some of it as it pertains to his observations:

> I have seen, the desperation and disorder of the powerless: how it twists the lives of children on the streets of Jakarta or Nairobi in much the same way as it does the lives of children on Chicago's South Side, how narrow the path is for them between humiliation and untrammeled fury, how easily they slip into violence and despair. (Obama, 2006, pp. x–xi)

With this in mind, on the flip side of oppression are forms of privilege, both for Obama and myself. With grandparents willing to struggle so their future investments (kids) would not experience similar oppressive forms of discrimination, our immediate parents put into motion forms of education that allowed social access. For me personally, although I dropped out of a private Jewish day school, my hardworking parents had the financial wherewithal to help pay for my future education when I was ready for it. From the roots of oppression as well, Obama's grandmother in particular instilled a hard-nosed work ethic into Obama that saw him eventually land at Harvard. What I have learned about privilege is that it is far easier to comment on social ills from a comfortable armchair and fireside than from the pit of despair in inner-city poverty, from the university classroom than from the steel mills, and so on. Access to knowledge was a privilege, and both Obama and I in our own worlds had lots of it. One element of this struggle of the tightrope between discrimination and privilege, it seems, is summed up by Obama (2006) when he comments on the relationship between one's history and that implied social access and one's responsibility to it:

> And what was a more interior, intimate effort on my part, to understand this struggle and to find my place in it, has converged with a broader public debate, a debate in which I am professionally engaged, one which will shape our lives and the lives of our children for many years to come. (p. xi)

I resonate with Obama's historical roots, if only symbolically. The movement from the recollection of those dangerous memories to social entrée has certainly tainted my philosophy of education, let alone my philosophy of life. Such questions arise: If one believes in social justice, how can one seriously engage in changing forms of oppression when one is hegemonized into privilege? What role do I play in my place of employment given the above conundrum, if at all? Is lip service only paid? Have we all been institutionally deceived into thinking about social justice but really enacting pure privilege? These questions drive my next section, which relates Obama's democratic dialogue in the face of institutional constraints.

From the Family Roots to Theory and Real Practice: Riding the Contradiction of the Market Logic versus Democratic Spaces

> I would agree that part of the hidden curriculum of the current structure and organization of education is bringing the marketplace, corporatization and business into the university and into schooling. (Margolis, 2001, p. 29)

> What is the task of educators at a time when the forces of democracy appear to be in retreat and the emerging ideologies and practices of militarization, corporatism and political fundamentalism bear down on every aspect of individual and collective experience? (Giroux, 2010, p. 232)

These quotes, although a decade apart, bear witness to the kind of dilemma educators are constantly faced with: the hidden curriculum of market forces on the rise and their impeding our everyday activities, whether in universities or public schools. As Giroux (2010) constantly reminds us, there are no simple solutions to these dilemmas other than to open up spaces for dialogue and critical thought.

With this in mind—in theory anyway—Obama's much-heralded visits to community events through town gatherings, his humanness as defined by his unique family history, his intellectual savvy, his willingness to fight for health for every American, and so on, bode well for education reform and potential democratic practice. However, the choice of Arne Duncan as Secretary of Education largely meant that Obama was to embrace and enhance the Bush administration's view of educational reform through high-stakes testing, increase the militarization of public schools, and decrease parent and community control of schools (Kumashiro, 2009). This emphatically included far more testing (Ravitch, 2009), stricter accountability measures, and a larger investment of charter schools. Rewards for poorer school performers were to be given in a real financial sense with the states' fight for "Race to the Top" dollars, awarded for increased achievement. Here in Indiana, school budgets have been viciously cut, and good teachers and other school folk are losing their jobs. (This is also happening extensively across the nation.) It is not difficult to surmise that the structural moves to cut budgets and job losses are linked to school districts being forced to return to the basics to increase test scores and throw out anything not linked to increasing student and school achievement. In short, the hidden curriculum of a rigid and uncompromising testing philosophy has been used to once again deskill teachers by reducing them to what Giroux and Saltman (2010) describe as "mere technicians," where students are "reduced to customers in the market place rather than engaged, critical learners" (p. 1).

Perhaps more important is the larger picture of Obama and Duncan, who mouth a good democratic talk on the one hand, but let a market-driven mind-set steer their philosophy on the other. For instance, Obama pursues the notion of what he defines as community charter schools, yet he does so within the language of increased "choice" and "competition" (Obama, 2008). Walking the tightrope by awarding teachers and schools bonuses for performance is pitted against Obama's critique of too much testing in the No Child Left Behind reform bill. Simply put, Obama's view toward increased testing and accountability for better achievement can be coupled to the economic views that place the United States in a struggle with India and China, whose students are better educated and better equipped to be successful in what Obama (2008) describes as the "knowledge economy." Eerily echoed here is the "Nation at Risk" reform, in which increasing standards is connected by a competitive mind-set to other countries, thereby involving increased human investment in education within a capital economy. The link between education and the economy reeks in all of Obama's (2005, 2007, 2008) educational talks. The above link between education and the economy is colored by the Obama administration's talk and subsequent action to make college more financially accessible and to prepare students in general to be better and more critical thinkers.

It is quite clear now that Obama's election did not guarantee swift educational reform. In my most optimistic moments, I leaned toward Obama's history of oppression and understanding of the complexity of difference and wondered whether he could trade this off for current oppressive educational policy. What I learned was that choosing an African American president gave hope to many people of color, to the voices of the obscured, and to the intellectuals as well. I also learned and hoped that progressive change had potential, that teacher unions were not shunned, and that the hope for audacity could rise. What I also learned was to ask the fundamental question: Could Obama give up these tests, the rigid accountability that simply stifles and deskills teachers, the overt commitment to school choice, excessive competition, and merit pay, and so on? Perhaps walking the line of the previous administration's educational policies and reinforcing them while straddling the line of democratic talk through community engagement and difference seeking and acceptance are what Anyon (2005) describes as radical possibilities for education. Could Obama and his administration go there? Or could there be possible outlets to test these waters? It is toward answers to these questions that I lead in the next sections.

Toward a Renewed Public Identity

In essence, Obama's election was a symbolic call for a renewed public identity. In my mind, a vision for a public identity has the potential to link personal history to subsequent action. Clearly, public identity calls for community action in the face of harsh economic times. At the heart of this renewed public identity, however, is the problematic marriage of a corporate school logic with its attendant testing practices, rigid accountability standards, and economic race for dollar gain, against the backdrop and belief and elation of racial tolerance, hope for a new potential with service to and for the public good spearheading new and invigorating prospects. This, among other things, is what the Obama administration with its figurehead president elevated inspired many to dream about.

Despite the "yes we can" language Obama used in his campaign, and my own leadership position at the university, the university's and public schools' public identity mirrors that of the corporate models described earlier. Judgment is for the most part based on the ideological notion of individualism—basing one's worth on specific accomplishments. Here in my workplace, for instance, tenure and promotion are largely determined by numbers of publications, graded teacher evaluations, and dollar grant acquisitions. Although I do not want to underplay the importance of establishing a personal professional identity in the academy, it seems to me that lost within the prior ideological logic of individualism is the language of the public good—selfless work that is not often rewarded done by folk who give generously of their time to their communities. Also, within university structures, although the language of public good and even social justice is mentioned on occasion—particularly in the Colleges of Arts and Sciences as well as Schools of Education and Fine Arts—more credence is given to class size, credit hours generated, and retention rates rather than what the universities perhaps are more centrally supposed to be about (that is, helping change communities for the public good, and this despite the structural importance of size, dollars, and credit hours just mentioned). Put differently, I do not buy into the argument that simply making dollars, acquiring more grants, growing a student body, or increasing retention rates is a movement away from a corporate model unless it is linked intimately to the quality of life in the community that these numbers could represent.

With this in mind, a renewed public identity in the education realm, whether at universities or public schools, means more than educating potential teachers and/or citizens to become "transformative intellectuals," as Giroux (1988) called them: those committed to challenging oppressive school structures through action and critical understanding of when to act. A renewed public identity is about the ability to imagine social justice and build what Cornel West (1993) describes as a prophetic public intellectualism. Here, one's personal history is linked to informed decision making, where transcending the contradiction of corporate logic and democratic and community struggle and activism requires the courage to act audaciously (Batagiannis, 2007). In other words, it would not be the Audacity of Hope that Obama calls for but what I am calling the Hope for Audacity. Perhaps in my world this is the ability to know not only when to act but how to act as well. Indeed, this may mean the dialogue of how to transcend publication numbers as a dominant form of evaluation and to view community action as a viable means for judgment—or in the public school sense, to know that Title 1 schools could be doing an incredible job with their students despite the low achievement numbers on standardized test scores. It may mean looking at grant work and seeing how it is linked to the public good. It may also mean looking at professional development schools as linked to community growth, not simply as delivery of goods and services between universities and public schools, such as simply marking off the number of in-services schools conduct, and so on. It seems to me that the ideological individualism line would be challenged by what I will label a "collectivism of the future." This collectivism, whether in the university community or public school community, will base decisions that are not top-down, as in a corporate model. Given that I am dean of a College of Education and Public Policy, I also know that decisions sometimes must be made top-down, if not just for practical purposes. Yet a public intellectualism needs to broaden or have the potential to broaden the participation of citizens in choices. The top-down model must be challenged not only for the public good but also for the health and well-being of the participating citizens in the community. Public discussion such as "Valuing individualism but not being a slave to its philosophy" could guide healthy dialogue at all levels. Clearly, Obama's conundrum (pitting national economic interests based on a philosophy of individualism against personal human value concerns which are not based on the economy or individual gain) is not dissimilar to mine, one that links history of experience of difference to public good can become seriously compromised within a corporate mind-set. The audacity and courage to challenge the ideological lines of the corporate model logic need community support and a prophetic vision that looks at timeless values such as selflessness, dignity, courage, and grace as guiding principles for subsequent evaluation and community growth. Those interested in struggling through the contradictions mentioned in this chapter certainly have work to do. In my conclusion, I outline some of the areas that may need investigating as we move forward to a renewed public identity.

Conclusion: Some Practical Questions and Concerns

In thinking about how a collective public identity relates pragmatically, certain practical issues come to mind. I first think about how colleges and schools of education are forced to link their work to accountability standards both internally, through accreditation agencies, and externally, to public schools and their struggle with institutional deskilling. Recently at Indiana University-Purdue University Fort Wayne (IPFW), a group of faculty completed a collective volume on the accreditation process (Swim et al., 2010). The struggle to talk beyond a corporate logic and above standardization and to meaningfully engage in discussion resulting from the book meant dealing with historical issues of the workforce, gender concerns, deskilling versus reskilling processes, and so on. In thinking beyond corporatism, I believe that we have to view a renewed vision of field placements—ones that are not simply technical assignments but are connected to service learning to the community in which one is placed. Perhaps that means viewing students as part of a 2–4 year placement, nestling themselves into a community, serving selflessly as they gain their credentials. Community work, service, and understanding and involvement override individual gain or a corporate logic, even though that logic is already embedded into school structures at the local, state, and federal levels. On a curricular level, schools of education cannot continue to describe themselves simply as "professional school" if they want to make inroads into the community. Linking schools of education with social causes—prisons, health institutions, environmental issues, and many more—means broadening the role of the school of education beyond that of a one-trick pony through which teachers are prepared for the workforce in limited methodological and quick ways. Clearly, it seems, a renewed public collective identity is the challenge of the linear role of schools of education and conducting internal discussion on how to do so.

At a local university level, I would like to see how a corporate promotion and tenure philosophy is challenged and thereby broadened to include the public good as a qualitative and revered item for consideration. Or, linking publication to community impact may need to be seriously investigated. For instance, a particular faculty may have written only one or two seminal articles, but perhaps their work impacted communities in far larger ways than the faculty who has written 30 published articles. Taking this logic further, how grant acquisition affects the public becomes paramount and equal to or stronger than the sum of the grant itself. Or, how retention rates increase as a result of community growth needs to be viewed and researched, rather than simply collecting retention rates as a marker for a university's funding equation. Or, how faculty simply use their time locally to aid the community rather than use time as an individualistic logic to simply advance careers needs to be viewed through a new lens in terms of adjudicating faculty production.

It seems to me that a renewed community and collective public identity also needs to view how one's personal voice interacts with the community. The concept of "voice" refers to the subjective element of the self.[2] How one's personal history—or, simply put, one's "dangerous memory"—plays out in a professional way needs to be deepened so that individualism can be challenged and transformed into community action. On a personal level, I am clearly a culprit in the system. I, too, have been hegemonized into a corporate logic that has placed more value on achievement than on public renewal. What I do not want to underplay in any professional career is that achievement. Yet I also know that with the current corporate mentality so pervasive, unless we take action to counter it, we may also fall prey to President Obama's powerful lingo. In other words, at least in the educational sense, we can get caught up in the president's eloquence at the expense of authentic challenges to the logic and subsequent ideology that Obama has really supported. To reiterate, our president has supported the kind of rigid testing and accountability frameworks that others and I have connected to a broader corporate-like, market mentality. He has also provided hope for challenging this consciousness by engaging the nation in the idea that the community and service could still win the day. However, it is the former ideology that has generally been put into practice. I do think our community of educators has to move beyond critique and toward action plans, some of which I have mentioned in this chapter. Clearly, a lot of think-tank and practical work needs to be accomplished so as to view and eventually alter ideological structures in order to operate in new and enlightening ways. I firmly believe we have no choice but to do so, because the current logic is crippling our collective identity and creativity. Yes we can!

Notes

Chapter One

1 For this chapter, I move broadly between using both university and public school sites as examples of the kinds of theoretical and practical dilemmas I discuss, particularly as related to the corporate model logic. A renewed public identity can and should be linked to both sites. I blur the boundaries of both these sites mainly because I see my work in the university and as dean as intimately linked to public schools and the issues that arise concurrently quite similar.

2 For more on the concept of voice, see Kanpol (1999).

References

Anyon, J. (2005). *Radical possibilities: Public policy, urban education and a new social movement.* New York: Routledge.

Batagiannis, S. (2007). Leadership guided by courage: A challenge to instantaneous perfection. *Journal of Educational Thought*, *41*(2), 145–164.

Giroux, H. (1988). *Teachers as intellectuals: Toward a critical pedagogy of learning*. Granby, MA: Bergin & Garvey.

———. (2010). Challenging the military-industrial-academic complex after 9/11. *Policy Futures in Education*, *8*(2), 232–237.

Giroux, H. & Saltman, K. (2010). *Obama's betrayal of public education: Arne Duncan and the corporate model of schooling*. Available at http://www.truthout.org/121708R?print

Grossberg, L. (1992). *We gotta get out of this place: Popular, conservative and postmodern culture.* New York: Routledge.

Kanpol, B. (1999). *Critical pedagogy: An introduction.* Westport, CT: Bergin & Garvey.

———. (2002). Critical educational leadership: Put up or shut up! *Educational Foundations*, *16*(1), 5–18.

Kumashiro, K. (2009, January 12). Wrong choice for secretary of education: A dissenting voice from Chicago. *Education Week.* Available at http://www.edweek.org/ew/articles/2009/01/12/18kumashiro-com.h28.html

Margolis, E. (Ed.). (2001). *The hidden curriculum of higher education.* New York: Routledge.

Obama, B. (1995). *Dreams from my father: A story of race and inheritance.* New York: Three Rivers Press.

———. (2005, October 25). *Teaching our kids in a 21st century economy*. Speech delivered to the Center for American Progress. Available at http://obama.senate.gov/speech/05105-teaching_our_ki/

———. (2006). *The audacity of hope: Thoughts on reclaiming the American dream.* New York: Random House.

———. (2007, November 7). *Our kids, our future*. Speech delivered in Manchester, NH. Available at http://www.barackobama.com2007/11/20/remarks_of_senator_barack_obam_34.php

———. (2008, May 28). *What's possible for our children*? Speech delivered in Thornton, CO. Available at http://www.denverpost.com/news/ci_9405199

Ravitch, D. (2009, June 15). *Obama gives Bush a 3rd term in education*. Available at http://www.commondreams.org?view/2009/06/15-9

Swim, T.J., Nichols, J.D., Murphey, K., Moss, G., Merz, A., Lindquist, D., & Kanpol, B. (2010). *Teacher National Accreditation as community dialogue: Transformative reflections.* Cresskill, NJ: Hampton Press.

Welch, S. (1990). *A feminist ethic of risk.* Minneapolis, MN: Fortress Press.

West, C. (1993). *Prophetic reflections: Notes on race and power in America*. Monroe, ME: Common Courage Press.

❖ CHAPTER TWO ❖

The First Step toward School Reform: Building Alliances of Consent through Deliberative Democracy

Kathleen A. Murphey

President Obama,

I believe in your presidency and the hope of progressive public policies that you have brought to the office. You have faced, and are facing, many complex and difficult policy decisions. Confronting them has meant building coalitions in Congress to pass progressive legislation. I admire your courage and talents at taking on these challenges. I ask, however, that you build coalitions with us, with educators, too. Even as we prepare teachers and school administrators to be leaders, we need your leadership, for the schools and our professions are perceived to be in crisis. We beseech you to reconsider your current school reform policy, as articulated in Race to the Top (2009) and *A Blueprint for Reform* (U.S. Department of Education, 2010), and redirect it as described below.

Your book *The Audacity of Hope: Thoughts on Reclaiming the American Dream* (2006) has inspired me to write to you about my dream, like yours, of educating *all* children to reach their highest potential with the hope of participating meaningfully in our democracy and, in the long run, furthering our democracy. You argue that we need a "'deliberative democracy' in which all citizens are required to engage in a process of testing their ideas against an external reality, persuading others of their point of view, and building shifting alliances of consent" (p. 92). I'd like to persuade you to consider my point of view. As a teacher educator and former high school teacher, I believe the goal of education, through schooling, should be to bring students, teachers, administrators, parents, teacher educators, and community members into that deliberative democracy.

You also say that our democracy is not "a house to be built, but…a conversation to be had" (p. 92). Currently, a deliberative, democratic conversation about schooling does not exist. It has disappeared from the public narrative about school reform. If there were a discussion, it would show little consensus, especially among current educators. I document that dissent below. Teachers, administrators, and teacher educators feel they have been ignored in the reform process, for the reforms threaten their professions at their core. These educators struggle with self-doubt as they question how they could have committed their lives to teaching but now appear to be blamed for the perceived crisis in P–12 student learning, which is being measured by very questionable high-stakes tests.[1] Teachers and teacher educators have been working hard to meet ever-higher standards; they see themselves as being on the front lines of educational reform; they see themselves, also—and unfortunately—on the front lines of criticism and blame for school and student failure. I seek to understand this misunderstanding and try to explain it to you. I seek to ask you to redirect your policies and work with the professionals who have been committed for years to help all children learn.

The No Child Left Behind Act (NCLB, 2001) has narrowed the debate, such as it is, to P–12 students' success or failure on high-stakes tests. Some students are achieving on these tests, but many are not. Race to the Top (2009) has further narrowed or cut off the discussion about educational reform by imposing an answer from above that eschews discussion by the concerned parties. It builds on excessive competition for federal dollars, which only a few states will receive. The winners will gain; the losers will have to make do at a time in which states are struggling with declining tax revenues that result in massive cuts in school funding, which in turn lead to school closings and teacher layoffs. Clearly, it seems that Race to the Top funds will take care of the lost revenue for a few states and, at the same time, force draconian changes in the delivery of education through such things as reconstitution of failing schools. Educators worry about the long-term consequences of this kind of winner-take-all system for funding education at the federal level. Educators—P–12 teachers, administrators, and teacher educators—feel as though they are standing on quicksand as they experience daily their respective professions being disparaged and their jobs being put on the line.

While there is no apparent deliberative, democratic discussion about the reforms, throughout the media there is a narrative of perceived failure—of students, teachers, administrators, and teacher educators. This inaccurate narrative of failure distracts from social, political, and economic challenges, especially in impoverished communities—challenges that need to be addressed concomitantly with saving "failing" schools and leading them to success. Schools are not islands; they exist in communities. Urban, suburban, and rural school districts often face different obstacles to success that are directly related to demographic and economic contexts of their respective communities. In any of those settings, schools can be destabilized by economic impoverishment, lack of jobs, new immigrants who don't yet speak English, and several competing ethnic cultures vying for their share of jobs and social services (Kozol, 1991, 2006). Additionally, students' high mobility from school to school and the high turnover of teachers, principals, and superintendents further challenge these communities (Kukla-Acevedo, 2009; Schafft, 2006; Smethem, 2007).

Thus, in spite of the narrative of "failure," which alternately blames students, teachers, administrators, teacher educators, or parents, it seems that the driving force of failure is actually a local "failing" economy. The economy in these communities with "failing" schools has been Left Behind. The dynamic sectors of the economic system have moved on or were never there in the first place. Thus, now we have Left Behind kids, by Left Behind teachers, trained by Left Behind teacher educators, all trying not to be Left Behind in their communities, which have been Left Behind by the forces of economic development. Instead of targeting schools, the media and the Department of Education should be studying the whole community. They should be analyzing how local economic failure and failing schools are impacted by new directions in the global economy and changing relationships between the state and the global economy. Communities, especially impoverished communities, lack visions for economic development that include their schools, and they lack the tools to pull themselves out of poverty.

With this narrative of "failure" in mind, privatized schools, or charter schools, which seek to avoid the devastation of failing local economies, will not touch the heart of the problem, the economic malfunctioning of local communities and school demise within that context. Privatized teacher training, which is targeting certain high-need subject areas such as math and science, will also not solve the problem of basic economic inequalities or foster the greater political goal of a deliberative democracy that you so eloquently articulate. To build alliances of consent, students, teachers, administrators, parents, and teacher educators need to deliberate solutions for our failing schools and failing communities. We need to work with one another to build vibrant schools that function in tandem with socially, politically, and economically functioning communities.

It seems to me and to many other educators that we need a high-stakes discussion by all stakeholders to analyze the problem and collaboratively address our multiple and complex educational challenges. Educators, especially, need to be drawn into these deliberations. We need a truly deliberative democracy in action so we can negotiate alliances of consent. We need you, Mr. President, to be part of that deliberative process, which you have stated you believe in. Current educational reforms, like many failed educational reforms of the past,[2] are trying to reform schools that we are told are "failing" without reforming the social and economic problems that lead to school "failure," without articulating the complex relationship between educational reform and the political economy, and without consulting educators. We, along with you, should deliberate these issues so that together we can become an alliance for reenvisioning, reshaping, and restoring our public schools. This should be the first step in building school reform.

Beginning the Deliberative Process

I turn now to educators, who express their concerns about current reforms, deliberating on issues I have raised above. They try to understand the role of (a) expectations, (b) community contexts, (c) changes in school governance, (d) segregation by social class and race, and (e) new economic forces, as variables impact the effectiveness of school reform policies.

Understanding Expectations

Rethinking Schools (2008), an educational publication that addresses issues in schools and is "firmly committed to equity and to the vision that public education is central to the creation of a humane, caring, multiracial democracy,"[3] was ecstatic over your election in 2008.

> Your historic victory and the increased mandate for change in Congress open up possibilities for serious changes in federal education policy. For progressive educators and advocates, we were excited to hear you state early in your campaign that "it's time to stop working against our teachers and start working with them. Teachers don't go into education to get rich....They want our children to succeed, but we've got to give them the tools. Invest in early childhood education. Invest in our teachers and our children will succeed." (pp. 4–6)

A year later, the editors of *Rethinking Schools* (2009) questioned why you were not turning to communities as you did during your organizing days in Chicago. They questioned your uncritical support of standardized tests, and they questioned your continued support of market-driven reforms promoted through NCLB:

> [T]here is a disturbing overlap between Obama's educational policies and those of George W. Bush—including an undiminished, and largely uncritical, commitment to standardized tests and charter schools; a continuing failure to address profound funding inequities between school districts; and a zestful invocation of schooling as a weapon of global economic competition. The new Title I School Improvement guidelines propose investing millions in strategies like the wholesale replacement of school staff ("reconstitution") and turning over schools to for-profit education management organizations. These top-down policies have no track record of success as school improvement strategies. They are more likely to seriously weaken the public system. (pp. 5-7)

The following year the editors noted excessive teacher bashing in the press:

> Spurred by the June 2 deadline for the second round of Race to the Top, states have raced to fire more teachers, tie pay and evaluation to student test scores, close or reconstitute more schools, and disempower teachers' unions and teaching as a profession trampling teachers, students, and communities in the process. (*Rethinking Schools*, 2010)

The push to eliminate tenure is a ruse, they claim, for eliminating "bad" teachers. They acknowledge that there are teachers who shouldn't be in the classroom, but tenure isn't the problem:

> Tenure is not a guaranteed job for life; it's the right, which all employees deserve, not to be fired without due process and without just cause. If the goal were really better teaching, Race to the Top would be promoting union/district peer review and mentoring programs that are effective in helping struggling teachers and removing those who can't make the grade. (*Rethinking Schools*, 2010)

The direction of your reform policies also worries urban education expert Pedro Noguera (2010), who states: "Market-based reforms like performance pay for teachers, the excessive emphasis on charter schools as alternatives to traditional public schools and the distribution of federal funds—once treated as entitlements to compensate for poverty—through competitive grants all represent a disturbing continuity with the policies of the past" (p. 11).

Teachers' unions have been fighting your efforts to reconstitute schools and to impose merit pay as states put pressure on them to make changes necessary to be eligible to apply for Race to the Top funds. At the July 2010 annual meetings of both the National Education Association (NEA) and the American Federation of Teachers (AFT), you or representatives from the Department of Education (DOE) were not scheduled to speak, "partly because union officials feared that administration speakers would face heckling," thereby indicating your administration's "strained relations" with two of your "most powerful political allies" (Dillon, 2010, July 5, p. A8). In response, Secretary of Education Arne Duncan claimed, "I have great respect for the leadership of both unions....We're trying to push a lot of change, and we've seen extraordinary breakthroughs in the last 18 months. But we won't agree on every issue" (p. A8).

Teachers would like to be your "powerful political allies," but it is difficult when your policies seem targeted against them and their professional associations. Meanwhile, as reforms initiated by the Race to the Top competition are becoming reality, the heated debate over them continues, especially the evaluation of teachers tied to student test scores and reconstituting schools (Dillon, 2010, September 2). Teachers had and have high expectations for your administration. Educators want you to expect great things of them so they can continue to expect great things of you.

Understanding Community Contexts

Not only have you not met educators' high expectations for what your leadership would bring to education by turning policy away from the market-driven model, but the policies fail to acknowledge or address the out-of-school community contexts that impact student achievement, particularly in economically impoverished communities. Wayne Au (2009) charges that inequalities in student achievement, the noted "achievement gaps" among racial, ethnic, English-language learners, special education students, and students living in poverty, are *unequal by design*. Our sophisticated, ever-increasing assessment systems are validating the "zip code" effect (that is, test results that reflect the economic status of the local community). For all the testing and seeking to equalize achievements and close achievement gaps, achievement scores seem to reflect the fact that the inputs from the community—its economic level, its educational level, its community enrichment activities, its professional resources—make a dramatic difference in whether students are successful on high-stakes tests. Clearly, the fewer the inputs, the lower the high-stakes test scores. Thus, the test scores become a barometer of social class in a community and, possibly, a predictor of the students' class status in the future. The tests have the effect, as was noted thirty-five years ago in the recently reissued work of Samuel Bowles and Herbert Gintis (1976, 2011), of legitimizing failure and perpetuating social class differences. Au labels this the "standardization of inequality." Students' fears of testing, and the use of their high-stakes test scores to threaten teachers, do not—and cannot—empower students and teachers to overcome factors in the community that are beyond their control.

Au (2009) analyzes the complexities of how the social, cultural, political, and economic institutions work together to control achievement and, in effect, prevent some students from achieving—this despite the fact that the stated goals of educational reform, especially of NCLB, are to promote achievement of all students, particularly those in impoverished school communities who have traditionally populated low-achieving schools. Nonetheless, Au ends on a note of hope, saying that if schools can be "unequal by design," they can be "equal by design" (p. 145). But that redesign would need to address all the factors—social, political, and economic—that impact student achievement. It is in this area that we sorely need educational leadership and a deliberative democratic process. We need schools "equal by design." Let us work with you, and deliberate with you, to design such schools instead of perpetuating unequal ones.

David Berliner (2009a, 2009b) also writes about the out-of-school factors that lead to low test scores in poor communities. He asks, "Are teachers responsible for low achievement by poor students?" and concludes that

> harsh social policies and the pernicious effects of poverty are more responsible for the problems we see in our schools than are teachers and administrators. That is, the problems of achievement among America's poor are much more likely to be located outside the school than in it. (Berliner, 2009a, p. 19)

Several "outside-of-school" factors converge to impact student achievement in poor communities: poor health care, food insecurity, pollution, family violence, and unsafe neighborhoods. Poor children often come to school unhealthy, hungry, or malnourished, suffering from mercury or lead poisoning, and having experienced violence at home or in the neighborhood. These factors constrain student learning no matter how hard teachers and administrators try to mitigate their impact. Berliner charges, as I do above, that placing blame for student failure on teachers and administrators avoids requiring the federal government to confront out-of-school factors that so clearly jeopardize P–12 students living in poverty. To teachers and administrators who work in these schools, it is clear that these factors need to be addressed if P–12 students are going to be able to achieve at a higher level. Again, you need to deliberate with educators to shape reforms that acknowledge and directly address the community factors that constrain P–12 students' learning.

Linda Darling-Hammond (2010a) underscores Berliner's argument. She criticizes our nation's decreasing support for education for children living in poverty, as the title of her recent book attests, *The Flat World and Education: How America's Commitment to Equity Will Determine Our Future.* Further, many of these children are at risk of ending up in the prison system. Most inmates are school dropouts, are functionally illiterate, and do not have the skills to compete successfully for a job. A growing prison population is a tragedy in itself, but it is a consequence of a failed education system that hits students in impoverished communities particularly hard (Darling-Hammond, 2010b, p. 15). Her prescription for taking "the education of poor children as seriously as we take the education of the rich" (p. 18) is to make investments in children's welfare:

> As in high- and equitably achieving nations, it would require strong investments in children's welfare—adequate healthcare, housing and food security, so that children can come to school each day ready to learn; high-quality preschool to close achievement gaps that already exist when children enter kindergarten; equitably funded schools that provide quality educators and learning materials, which are the central resources for learning. (Darling-Hammond, 2010b, p. 18)

For Darling-Hammond (2010a, 2010b), Race to the Top focuses on "peripheral" issues and does not commit to long-term investments that would make a difference:

> The implementation of Race to the Top has not required states to equalize funding to underresourced schools or even to maintain their existing commitments to these schools, many of which have had to slash budgets deeply, laying off tens of thousands of teachers, raising class size to more than forty in some cases and cutting successful programs. (p. 18)

Her recommendation for those schools that serve poor children is to set up a community school system that provides social, cultural, health, pre- and after-school programs, and other human services to students in addition to a rigorous academic curriculum.

Au, Berliner, and Darling-Hammond all agree that out-of-school factors have to be taken very seriously, if not more seriously, than in-school factors. Rather than blaming educators and instituting market-driven reforms, we should be directly addressing community contextual variables that, if ignored, will continue to stymie school reform.

Understanding Changes in School Governance

Educational historian Diane Ravitch (2010a, 2010b) repudiates her longstanding support of NCLB testing and accountability measures. She joins the rising chorus of educators who critique the current educational reforms. She chronicles her developing views and reveals the inner workings of administrative reformers from her personal conversations with those reformers. She is most critical of the new management and leadership of school systems that have been taken out of the hands of educators and are in the process of being turned over to MBAs and lawyers who support a top-down business model of leadership. Perhaps most surprising and pleasing to her former critics is that she strongly supports teachers and their ability to deliver the curriculum because the new managers have no expertise in, or understanding of, curriculum. Teachers and teacher educators have responded warmly to her book *The Death and Life of the Great American School System: How Testing and Choice Are Undermining Education* (Ravitch, 2010a). It was sold out within a week of publication and has gone through multiple printings to keep up with demand. Although her critique is not new to many educational scholars, who share her current views, it was new that she had changed "sides." Her targeted support of teachers and their professional skills was also new, which had the effect on teachers and administrators of an elixir, so seldom do they hear praise. According to Ravitch, it is not just that teachers should not be blamed for alleged student failure, as Au, Darling-Hammond, and Berliner so eloquently state, but they should be honored for the knowledge and pedagogical skills they possess, particularly because the "measure and punish" assessment approach of NCLB and Race to the Top is no guarantee that the curriculum will be learned.

One of Ravitch's chapters (2010a), "The Billionaire Boys Club," has drawn particular attention because it critiques and chronicles the recent history of how wealthy foundations are determining many reforms in education, as they bring tremendous financial resources to challenges in the educational arena that public dollars are unable to provide. These organizations, such as the Bill and Melinda Gates Foundation, the Walton Family Foundation, and the Eli and Edythe Broad Foundation, have no public oversight; they have no one to be accountable to.[4] Thus, Ravitch argues that the business model has taken over in large school corporations, and some of the leading reforms are being financed without public oversight. In the business model, teachers have no voice. Race to the Top reinforces this market-driven model because it encourages charter schools, which are often offshoots of national, for-profit companies; seeks to break the teachers' unions; and encourages outsourcing of some of the functions of public school systems. Ravitch is most critical of the fact that a rigorous curriculum, which she has always supported, has not been revised or supported through federal policy, think-tank policy, or foundations. She contends that the corporate, market-oriented, business model of top-down, hierarchical control is inimical to the purposes of schooling.

Understanding Segregation by Social Class and Race

Some scholars feel that the answer to inequalities in the schools related to social class, which result in low achievement scores by some students, is to integrate schools by social class. Gerald Grant (2009), for example, puts forward the example of Raleigh, North Carolina, in his *Hope and Despair in the American City: Why There Are No Bad Schools in Raleigh.* In 1976, "without any court order, the Raleigh city and county schools merged to create the Wake County School System" (p. 97). As the various neighborhoods included homeowners from all social classes, each subsection of the city educates the children of the rich, the poor, and the middle classes and children of all ethnicities and races. Middle-class parents make demands on the schools that parents of children of the poor haven't made as strongly in the past; all children benefit by getting the same high-quality education. Although current changes in the school board have put this program in jeopardy, Grant sees this as a model for improving the system we now have, where students from poor neighborhoods do not get a first-class education. Now schools, particularly urban schools, are experiencing hypersegregation by both race and class (Au, 2009; Flinspach & Banks, 2009). Grant's model addresses both. He concludes that this is not about test scores:

> It's about the kind of nation we hope to become. We should not want, nor shall we ever achieve, a nation of equal test scores or equal incomes. But we do need to decide whether we want schools segregated by race and class, or schools that provide equal educational opportunity for all children—schools where students are enriched by relationships and ways of thinking that help them break out of the boxes of race and class that our flawed history has constructed. (Grant, 2009, pp. 190–191)

It is difficult, however, to initiate economic integration in cities that have not had the kind of history Raleigh has had. Pauline Lipman and David Hursh look at similar attempts in Chicago to initiate mixed-income schools and housing and find that they have not worked. In fact, they seem to disadvantage poor neighborhoods even further (Lipman, 2008, 2011; Lipman & Hursh, 2007). These policies, which were designed to overcome housing and educational inequalities, have had the opposite effect. The researchers lay blame for this ineffectiveness on neoliberal political and economic policies that seek to privatize former public institutions, thereby disempowering public schools and the teachers and administrators who work in them.

Mr. President, from your deft descriptions in *The Audacity of Hope* of the political strengths and weaknesses of previous administrations, and from your chronicle of the history of free-market capitalism and the state's evolving regulation and deregulation of it,[i] it is clear that you understand the political and economic forces they speak of, although you don't name them. In fact, you see yourself as struggling over the balance between markets and democracy as growing inequality in wealth makes it harder for us to maintain our sense of "common kinship":

> More than anything, it is that sense—that despite great differences in wealth, we rise and fall together—that we can't afford to lose....Jefferson was not entirely wrong to fear Hamilton's vision for the country [which favored a strong national economy and fluid markets in capital (p. 151)], for we have always been in a constant balancing act between self-interest and community, markets and democracy, the concentration of wealth and power and the opening up of opportunity. (Obama, 2006, p. 193)

It is precisely this "balancing act" between "self-interest and community, markets and democracy" and "the concentration of wealth and power and the opening up of opportunity" that we feel is being played out in the schools.

We worry that the current educational reform policies put "community," "democracy," and "opportunity" at risk because the policies seem to reward "self-interest" and "markets" and increase "the concentration of wealth and power" rather than challenge it. We need to understand the economic and political forces that are tipping the balance in the wrong direction.

Understanding New Economic Forces

How do we understand this market-driven model as it emerges ever more visibly in the educational arena? The economic and political theory of neoliberalism fosters deregulation of businesses, privatization of former state functions, outsourcing, competition, individualism, and hierarchical top-down control, and it is anti-labor and anti-union. Insofar as schools are being run as businesses and by businesses, they are also built around profits. Federal policies—NCLB and Race to the Top—seem to be taking education out of the public sector, supported by public funds, and reinventing it in the private sector. As public funds get squeezed, federal funds for the neediest schools, meant to equalize opportunity for students on the margins, are being reduced. Thus, as the state seems to be in the process of turning over P–12 schooling to privatizers and foundations, public school systems are being weakened. This model, furthered by NCLB and Race to the Top policies, is being increasingly identified with the economic and political philosophy of neoliberalism,[6] which is an ideology currently driving global capitalist economic development. David Harvey (2005) explains:

> Neoliberalism is in the first instance a theory of political economic practices that proposed that human well-being can best be advanced by liberating individual entrepreneurial freedoms and skills within an institutional framework characterized by strong private property rights, free markets, and free trade....Furthermore, *if markets do not exist* (in areas such as land, water, *education*, health care, social security, or environmental pollution) *then they must be created*, by state action if necessary. But beyond these tasks the state should not venture. *State interventions in markets (once created) must be kept to a bare minimum*. (p. 2; italics added)

Businesses hoping to be successful view the neoliberal framework positively. Those of us who have spent our lives as students and as educators in the public sector struggle with this political/economic philosophy because we think education should not be marketized or privatized. We think it should remain in the public sector, and the public sector should remain a dynamic force.

The privatization of public workforces such as teachers has been advocated by many political conservatives, including Indiana's Republican governor Mitch Daniels (2006), in the name of "Reforming government through competition":

> The case for judicious private contracting rests, of course, not just on superior efficiency but also on grounds of sound philosophy: anything that strengthens the private sector vs. the state is protective of personal freedom. And in an economically struggling state like ours, channeling more public dollars to private businesses can make a modest contribution to a stronger economy.

Daniels claims that government employees are the "new privileged class in America" because of their reputed high salaries and good benefits, which their unions negotiated for them through collective bargaining. He argues that they are costly to the state, thus their work should be privatized (Smith, 2010). Daniels is but one of a growing group of conservatives who are targeting public employees as being too expensive for the public to finance (Traub, 2010). Race to the Top appears to support this anti-state-sector, pro-private-sector, anti-union perspective by introducing competition and merit pay into the pay scales of teachers and encouraging charter schools as an alternative to public schools. We question why Race to the Top seems to align so well with the governor's conservative, neoliberal views.

Hursh (2005, 2007, 2008) analyzes how NCLB expresses neoliberal policies that seek to make education efficient by measuring the product (that is, what students have learned and, in the end, whether students fail the tests) to justify converting them into a private alternative: "The aim of NCLB and other high-stakes testing reforms...may be less about improving student learning and closing the achievement gap than it is about undermining public education to introduce a market-based system" (Hursh, 2007, p. 504). Patricia Burch (2009) explains further in *Hidden Markets: The New Education Privatization*: "The new privatization is harnessed to those broader ideological shifts in theories of economic and political regulation that are referred to as neoliberalism" (p. 2). She documents how privatization has played a big role in the development and delivery of educational services, a role largely "hidden" from public view. She concludes that some private firms can play a role in education, but:

> Right now, the center of gravity in public policy is shifting. Ideologies of neoliberalism are remaking education policy to fit the needs of the market. The ideas are pushed as helping public education although the arguments have little empirical basis. (Burch, 2009, p. 136)

Although neoliberalism is a relatively new concept to most U.S. educators, it is not new to educators around the globe, where this economic and political philosophy has visibly spread into the educational arena—long thought to be immune from such forces—often with negative consequences to the educational labor force and to the students hoping to be educated. Neoliberalism has challenged the long-established traditions of teaching, learning, and school governance, especially as the privatization movement unbuilds public schools, demeans their traditional purpose of educating a democratic citizenry, and redefines the roles of teachers (Apple, 2009; Compton & Weiner, 2008; Macvrine, McLaren, & Hill, 2010).

A group of Australian teacher educators, for example, has felt the consequences of neoliberal policies in their country's economy and in the educational system, but they, like you, seek hope, and they, like you, seek a deliberative democracy. Sawyer et al. (2007) try to define "robust hope" and how one can achieve it, given policies that seem to be trying to destroy hope in the public educational arena. As they describe their project and detail how one can seek robust hope, they quote Aristotle, who wrote more than 2,000 years ago, when democracy was in its infancy, about the importance of education as a public, not a private, affair:

> No one would dispute the fact that it is a lawgiver's prime duty to arrange for the education of the young. In states where this is not done the quality of the constitution suffers....[S]ince there is but one aim for the entire state, it follows that education must be one and the same for all, and that the responsibility for it must be a public one, not a private affair....In matters that belong to the public, training for them must be the public's concern. (Aristotle, 1981, p. 452; quoted in Sawyer et al., 2007, p. 230)

Today's educators can't understand the educational "reform" policies, which they interpret as being against them and against the full development of children's cognitive, emotional, and social capacities, without understanding something about the evolving political economy, the forces of marketization, privatization, and the changing role of the state—all referred to as neoliberalism—and the impact it is having on the public sphere in which teachers, administrators, and teacher educators reside. Educators seek to—and need to—understand these powerful forces that, as they see it, are disrupting their lives, challenging their profession, working against children, and unbuilding the public sector. To reiterate forcefully, educators need to be part of the deliberative process that formulates workable educational reform policies that resist these new political/economic forces that threaten public education and a deliberative democracy.

President Obama,

Back to you. We as teachers and teacher educators need you back on our side. Please listen to our arguments. Please trust us and not let us be cast aside as our jobs become privatized and our professions maligned. You need us to do the jobs we've been doing to teach P–12 students and to train future teachers to meet the complex demands of the 21st century. In *The Audacity of Hope*, you seemed to understand the politics and economics of the world very well. Can you tell us, in all honesty, why these neoliberal policies will lead to a better educational system, especially if it isn't public? Can you tell us why we have been left out of the deliberative process? Could you help facilitate a public space to hold us, including you, to your promise of a deliberative process over the issues raised here?

In the summer of 2009, educator Gloria Ladson-Billings commented on the obstacles and opportunities that your administration faced. She took the liberty, supported by her own theoretical framework, of encapsulating her thoughts in an imaginary rendering of a meeting attended by you, Secretary of Education Arne Duncan, Secretary of the Treasurer Timothy Geithner, Vice President Joe Biden, and the rest of your cabinet 3 years after your inauguration. In this imagined scenario, Arne Duncan does not understand why his reforms have not worked. Explanations come from Secretary Geithner:

> [Y]ou never developed a vision for education in the new economy. You…never connected with the citizens….Teachers are a huge constituency. They are not just teachers. They are voters. They are parents. They are spouses. They are community members. They are one of our most populated professions. How far do you think we would have gotten on the auto bailout if we had attacked the autoworkers instead of the obscenely rich CEOs? (Ladson-Billings, 2009, p. 356)

Through this imagined discussion in the future, Ladson-Billings critiques Secretary Duncan for misreading the public school community and ignoring the concerns of the educational workforce. Duncan goes over their heads with market-driven, privatized alternatives and does so, as imagined here by Ladson-Billings, in ways that ultimately reduce any real impact on the current system. Will this imagined scene become reality next year?

Mr. President, P–12 teachers and teacher educators are getting the message loud and clear—as the tentacles of the Race to the Top policy reach local districts—that their jobs and professions are on the line. They are demoralized. The policies you support, and that Arne Duncan espouses, are going in the wrong direction. They are clearly not part of a deliberative process you seemed once to espouse. They are anti-labor and pro-business, and they support a market model driven by individual choice and competition, not a democratic model where all the participants in the schools' larger communities work together to educate the next generation of citizens and to create an educational system that is "equal by design." In the balance you seek between "free markets and democracy," current educational policies are favoring free markets at the expense of democracy, a deliberative democracy.

The Race to the Top dollars would be better invested in (a) school-community economic development in struggling communities; (b) grants to prospective teachers to complete rigorous teacher education programs in schools of education; (c) incentives to schools of education to integrate their teacher education more closely with local school districts; (d) incentives to teachers to teach in schools in impoverished communities; (e) incentives to teacher unions—yes, teacher unions—to bring their members on board with the changes necessary to reach all students and to use their collective power to rise to the challenge of re-visioning schools; (f) incentives to P–12 school faculty to collaborate with one another and with local community partners to build and sustain strong programs; and (g) incentives to community agencies and organizations to invest in the success of children in the local public schools. The goal of educational policy should be to reinvent struggling communities by encouraging local leadership to shape policies that build excellent schools and productive communities together. Educational policy and economic policy should be integrated into a vision for sustainable communities, sustainable schools, and—most important—a sustainable, democratic world.

Teachers are by and large a progressive force and strongly committed to the children they teach. They seek to be the excellent teachers everyone wants them to be, especially in the face of daunting conditions over which they have little control. Mr. President, you need them as a progressive force in your larger political agenda. Poverty is the main problem in the schools; it is not the teachers or the teacher educators. Neoliberal political and economic policies that promote privatization and the unbuilding of public school systems, not the millions of children who do not do well on narrowly constructed high-stakes tests, are also the problem. Please support policies that keep educators on your side. If not, they are ripe for resisting your current policies, which they increasingly view as inimical to broad educational goals. They support you and your leadership, but they want you to listen to them.

Let teachers, school administrators, and teacher educators help you lead. A market-driven model of competition, privatization, and outsourcing is enriching the pockets of the privatizers and eroding the vitality of public schools. It fosters top-down control with little respect for educators, who are doing the hard work of educating. It ignores the out-of-school factors that seriously undermine the possibility for success of schools in impoverished communities that serve mainly marginalized populations. With the dominance of high-stakes tests, little long-term knowledge will survive. The values of social interaction, democracy, critical perspective, and inclusivity have no space. The students may end up passing the tests, but they will be ignorant of much we depend on to enable our democracy to survive. We are, in effect, teaching ignorance—ignorance of the political and economic institutions and values that structure our society and its opportunities and responsibilities. And you are making teachers partners in this crime. You are privatizing hope when it needs to be democratized.

We hope that you can put privatization on hold and give public education a chance. We hope you can turn away from the neoliberal policies that you have put in motion for education and revitalize the public school model, which would partner, when necessary, with local community agencies and institutions to guarantee the success of all schools and all children. Privatization in its many forms is destroying our public schools. It is taking "the public" out of education. Let the teachers, administrators, and teacher educators lead in their respective arenas. Deliberate with us. Build with us, democratically, alliances of consent to reenvision, reshape, and restore our public schools as we take a first step toward school reform together.

Notes

Chapter Two

1 Many educators have raised serious questions about the use and value of high-stakes tests (see Berliner, 2006; Bracey, 2002; Glass, 2008; Hursh, 2008; Kohn, 2004; McNeil, 2000, 2002; Meier & Wood, 2004; Nichols & Berliner, 2007).

2 The effectiveness of educational reforms in the past has been much studied and debated by educational historians (see, e.g., Katz, 1968; Tyack & Cuban, 1995; Reese & Rury, 2008).

3 For more about the vision of *Rethinking Schools*, see http://www.rethinkingschools.org/about/index.shtml

4 For further elaboration of this argument see Kovacs (2011).

5 See Obama (2006), Chapters 1 and 5, respectively.

6 Neoliberalism (not to be confused with political liberalism) is perhaps best described as a rebirth of *economic* liberalism of the 19th century when free-market, unregulated capitalism first held sway, a model associated with classical economist Adam Smith. At the beginning of the 20th century, in response to the excessive wealth accumulation by capitalists and severe boom-and-bust cycles of the economy in the late 19th century, regulations were put into place by the state. By the 1930s, Keynesian economics, heralded by the New Deal, expanded the role of the state even more, so that the government could further regulate the economy and provide the social services that the free-market economy could not. By the 1980s, when the emerging globalized world economy was faltering, President Ronald Reagan ushered in what we now call neoliberal policies, which critiqued Keynesianism for excessive state expenditures that inhibited economic growth in the private sector. Reagan sought free markets, competition among private enterprises to ensure efficiency and high productivity, privatization and/or outsourcing of former state-supported services, a scaling back of worker wages, and antipathy to labor unions. These trends have been the driving forces in global economic development for the last 30 years. They were first articulated in the field of education by the *Nation at Risk* report (1983, April), which tied education to worker productivity within a global world economy. It has been most visible in the U.S. educational reform arena with the passage of NCLB in 2001. NCLB can be viewed as the neoliberal version of the Elementary and Secondary Education Act (ESEA) of 1965, which it replaced. Race to the Top appears to be built even more on this theory. It was the hope of educators, as noted earlier in this chapter, that your administration would turn away from these market-oriented policies in the field of education (see Apple, 2006, 2009; Au, 2009; Burch, 2009; Compton & Weiner, 2008; Gabbard, 2008; Giroux, 2004; Harvey, 2005; Hursh, 2005, 2008; Lipman, 2008, 2011; Lipman & Hursh, 2007; Robertson, 2000; Ross & Gibson, 2007).

References

Apple, M. (2006). *Educating the "right" way: Markets, standards, and inequality.* New York: Routledge.

———. (2009). *Global crises, social justice, and education.* New York: Routledge.

Au, W. (2009). *Unequal by design: High-stakes testing and the standardization of inequality.* New York: Routledge/Taylor & Francis Group.

Aristotle. (1981). *The politics* (rev. ed.). Harmondsworth, UK: Penguin.

Berliner, D.C. (2006). Our impoverished view of educational reform. *Teachers College Record, 108*(6), 949–995. Retrieved July 28, 2010, from http://www.tcrecord.org/content.asp?contentid=12106

———. (2009a, Fall). Are teachers responsible for low achievement by poor students? *Kappa Delta Pi Record*, pp. 18–21.

———. (2009b). *Poverty and potential: Out-of-school factors and school success.* Boulder, CO; Tempe, AZ: Education and the Public Interest Center, University of Colorado & Education Policy Research Unit, Arizona State University. Available at http://epicpolicy.org/publication/poverty-and-potential

Bowles, S., & Gintis, H. (1976). *Schooling in capitalist America: Educational reform and the contradictions of economic life.* New York: Basic Books.

———. (2011). *Schooling in capitalist America: Educational reform and the contradictions of economic life.* Chicago: Haymarket Books.

Bracey, G.W. (2002). *The war against America's public schools: Privatizing schools, commercializing education.* Boston: Allyn & Bacon.

Burch, P. (2009). *Hidden markets: The new education privatization.* New York: Routledge/Taylor & Francis Group.

Compton, M., & Weiner, L. (Eds.). (2008). *The global assault on teachers, teaching, and teacher unions: Stories for resistance.* New York: Palgrave Macmillan.

Daniels, M.E. (2006). *Reforming government through competition.* Los Angeles: The Reason Foundation. Retrieved June 22, 2010, from http://www.reason.org/apr2006/apr2006_daniels.shtml

Darling-Hammond, L. (2010a). *The flat world and education: How America's commitment to equity will determine our future.* New York: Teachers College Press.

———. (2010b, June 14). Restoring our schools: Forget quick fixes. To compete internationally, we need to improve the whole system. *The Nation, 290(23)*, 14–15, 17–20.

Dillon, S. (2010, July 5). New tension in Obama's tie to teachers. *The New York Times*, pp. A8, A11.

———. (2010, September 2). Formula to grade teachers' skill gains acceptance, and critics. *The New York Times*, p. A1. Retrieved September 2, 2010, from http://www.nytimes.com/2010/09/01/education/01teacher.html?_r=1&emc=eta1

Elementary and Secondary Education Act of 1965, Pub. L. 89-10.

Flinspach, S.L., & Banks, K.E. (2009). Moving beyond race: Socioeconomic diversity as a race-neutral approach to desegregation in the Wake County Schools. In J.C. Boger & G. Orfield (Eds.), *School resegregation: Must the South turn back*? (pp. 261–280). Chapel Hill: University of North Carolina Press.

Gabbard, D. (Ed.). (2008). *Knowledge & power in the global economy: The effects of school reform in a neoliberal/neoconservative age* (2nd ed.). New York: Lawrence Erlbaum Associates/Taylor & Francis Group.

Giroux, H. (2004). *The terror of neoliberalism: Authoritarianism and the eclipse of democracy.* Herndon, VA: Paradigm Publishers.

Glass, G.V. (2008). *Fertilizers, pills, and magnetic strips: The fate of public education in America.* New York: Information Age Publishing, Inc.

Grant, G. (2009). *Hope and despair in the American city: Why there are no bad schools in Raleigh.* Cambridge, MA: Harvard University Press.

Harvey, D. (2005). *A brief history of neoliberalism.* New York: Oxford University Press.

Hursh, D. (2005). Neoliberalism, markets, and accountability: Transforming education and undermining democracy in the United States and England. *Policy Futures in Education, 3*(1), 5–15.

———. (2007). Assessing No Child Left Behind and the rise of neoliberal education policies. *American Educational Research Journal, 44*(3), 493–518.

———. (2008). *High-stakes testing and the decline of teaching and learning: The real crisis in education.* Lanham, MD: Rowman & Littlefield.

Katz, M. (1968). *The irony of early school reform: Educational innovation in mid-nineteenth century Massachusetts*. Cambridge, MA: Harvard University Press.

Kohn, A. (2004, April). Test today, privatize tomorrow: Using accountability to "reform" public schools to death. *The Phi Delta Kappan, 85*(8), 568–577.

Kovacs, P.E. (Ed.). (2011). *The Gates Foundation and the future of U.S. "public" schools.* New York: Routledge.

Kozol, J. (1991). *Savage inequalities: Children in America's schools.* New York: Crown Publishers.

———. (2006). *The shame of the nation: The restoration of apartheid in schooling in America.* NewYork: Three Rivers Press.

Kukla-Acevedo, S. (2009). Leavers, movers, and stayers: The role of workplace conditions in teacher mobility decisions. *Journal of Educational Research, 102*(6), 443–452.

Ladson-Billings, G. (2009, Summer). Education for everyday people: Obstacles and opportunities facing the Obama administration. *Harvard Educational* Review, *79*(2), 345–359.

Lipman, P. (2008, March). Mixed-income schools and housing: Advancing the neoliberal urban agenda. *Journal of Educational Policy, 23*(2), 119–134.

———. (2011). *The new political economy of urban education: Neoliberalism, race, and the right to the city.* New York: Routledge.

Lipman, P., & Hursh, D. (2007). Renaissance 2010: The reassertion of ruling-class power through neoliberal policies in Chicago. *Policy Futures in Education*, *5*(20), 160–178.

Macvrine, S., McLaren, P., & Hill, D. (Eds.). (2010). *Revolutionizing pedagogy: Education for social justice within and beyond global neo-liberalism.* New York: Palgrave Macmillan.

McNeil, L.M. (2000). *Contradictions of school reform: Educational costs of standardized testing*. New York: Routledge.

———. (2002, Summer). Editor's introduction: Private asset or public good: Education and democracy at the crossroads. *American Educational Research Journal*, *39*(2), 243–248.

Meier, D., & Wood, G.H. (Eds.). (2004). *Many children left behind: How the No Child Left Behind Act is damaging our children and our schools.* Boston: Beacon Press.

National Commission on Excellence in Education. (1983, April). *A nation at risk: The imperative for educational reform.* A report to the nation and the secretary of education. Washington, DC: U.S. Department of Education.

Nichols, S.L., & Berliner, D.C. (2007). *Collateral damage: How high-stakes testing corrupts America's schools.* Cambridge, MA: Harvard University Press.

No Child Left Behind Act of 2001, Pub. L. No.109–110, 115 Stat. 1425 (2002).

Noguera, P. (2010, June 14). A new vision for school reform: The change we need in education policy. *The Nation*, *23*, 11–12, 14.

Obama, B.H. (2006). *The audacity of hope: Thoughts on reclaiming the American dream.* New York: Three Rivers Press.

Race to the Top. (2009, February 17). *Education Department: American Recovery and Reinvestment Act of 2009.* Retrieved July 5, 2010, from http://www2.cd.gov/policy/gcn/lcg /recovery/index.html

Ravitch, D. (2010a). *The death and life of the great American school system: How testing and choice are undermining education.* New York: Basic Books.

———. (2010b, June 14). Why I changed my mind: "Choice" and "accountability" sounded good on paper, but in reality, they have failed. *The Nation*, *290(23)*, 20–22, 24.

Reese, W.J., & Rury J.L. (Eds.). (2008). *Rethinking the history of American education.* New York: Palgrave Macmillan.

Rethinking Schools. (Eds.). (2008, Fall). An open letter to President-elect Obama. *Rethinking Schools*, *23*(1), 4–6.

———. (Eds.). (2009, Fall) Where is our community organizer-in-chief? *Rethinking Schools*, *24*(1), 5–7.

———. (Eds.). (2010, Summer). What's up with all the teacher bashing? *Rethinking Schools*, *24*(4). Retrieved June 19, 2010, from http://www.rethinkingschools.org/index.shtml

Robertson, S.L. (2000). *A class act: Changing teachers' work, the state, and globalization.* New York: Falmer Press.

Ross, E.W., & Gibson, R. (Eds.). (2007). *Neoliberalism and education reform.* Cresskill, NJ: Hampton Press.

Sawyer, W., Singh, M., Woodrow, C., Downes, T., Johnston C., & Whitton, D. (2007, August). Robust hope and teacher education. *Asia-Pacific Journal of Teacher Education, 35*(3), 227–242.

Schafft, K. (2006). Poverty, residential mobility, and student transiency within a rural New York school district. *Rural Sociology*, *71*(2), 212–231.

Smethem, L. (2007). Retention and intention in teaching careers: Will the new generation stay? *Teachers & Teaching*, *13*(5), 465–480.

Smith, B. (2010, June 6). *Going after public workers*. Retrieved July 5, 2010, from http://www.politico.com/blogs/bensmith/0610/Going_after_public_workers.html

Traub, A. (2010, July 5). War on public workers. *The Nation*, *291(1)*, 4–6.

Tyack, D., & Cuban, L. (1995). *Tinkering toward utopia: A century of public school reform.* Cambridge, MA: Harvard University Press.

U.S. Department of Education. (2010, March). *Blueprint for reform: The reauthorization of the elementary and secondary education act.* Alexandria, VA: Author. Retrieved August 20, 2010, from http://www2.ed.gov/policy/elsec/leg/blueprint/publicationtoc.html

❖ PART TWO ❖

OBAMA'S CURRENT LEADERSHIP

❖ CHAPTER THREE ❖

Deciphering the Narrative of School Failure: Misconceptions about Public School Reform

Jonathan C. Hilpert

One of the most common and prevalent narratives about public schools is the extensively unjustified and under-criticized notion that they are failing (Berliner & Biddle, 1995; Rothstein, 2004; Smith, 2004). Politicians, media organizations, journalists, special interest groups, educational entrepreneurs, and the like have widely advanced the notion that the American public education system is broken and in need of repair. So common is the narrative, and so prevalent is the notion that schools are failing, that few question the credibility, accuracy, or evidence underscoring the charge. Instead, many concern themselves with proposing drastic institutional reform focused on changing the nature of the institution rather than isolating and ameliorating specific problems (Molnar, 2002). However, radical changes such as the advancement of charter schools and school vouchers have not produced empirical evidence of success, are rationalized almost exclusively by ideology, and overshadow pragmatic reform efforts with great potential for success (Berliner, 2006; Bracey, 2003; Glass, 2008).

Dramatic structural reforms to public schools advanced by conservatives and neoliberals alike include the implementation of charter schools, vouchers, and so-called school choice. Other types of dramatic reform, such as the implementation of high-stakes testing or the micromanagement of standards, are based on the notion that public schools are beyond repair. However, there is much evidence to the contrary. For example, IQ scores have been on the rise for decades (Flynn, 1994), as have standardized test scores (Bracey, 2003). Scores for students' crystallized intelligence (learned information) and fluid intelligence (problem solving) have shown dramatic increases in the

United States (Flynn, 1994). Additionally, all six major ethnic categories used by the college board have shown dramatic increases on the Scholastic Aptitude Test (SAT), and similarly striking increases have been shown for all age groups, disaggregated by ethnicity, for the National Assessment of Educational Progress (NAEP), otherwise known as the "nation's report card" (Bracey, 2003). Additionally, middle- and upper-class students in our country score in the top three on internationally norm-referenced math, science, and reading tests such as the Trends in International Mathematics and Science Study (TIMSS) and the Program for International Student Assessment (PISA) (Berliner, 2006; Lemke et al., 2001). However, despite this and an abundance of other research-based, empirical evidence that suggests our public schools perform quite well, the common narrative surrounding public schools is that they are "failing."

In one often-cited and telling Gallup Poll (Phi Delta Kappa, 2001), respondents rated their children's schools as performing well but simultaneously reported that other children's schools were underperforming. Most students in the United States have access to educators who, by and large, work tirelessly to do their very best for students and make a positive impact. Nevertheless, many people are willing to entertain dramatic reform proposals, even those that cannot be supported with research or have been shown to be less effective than measures that can be implemented without dramatic change. Educational researchers have been able to isolate educational changes that are the most effective, but little political attention has been paid to these reforms. Instead they are often overshadowed by the dramatic systemic reform proposals mentioned earlier and rationalized by the under-criticized rhetoric of failing schools. The purpose of this chapter is to determine the source of the narrative of failing schools, why it is a dangerous narrative for teachers, and how it has overshadowed the educational reform efforts that have shown empirical evidence of success.

Social Reproduction and the Function of Public Schools

The success of U.S. teachers is not just overlooked; our social vision of education has been hijacked, and teachers' successes over the decades have been reframed as failures. Although American student success and growth have been demonstrated on norm-referenced tests such as the SAT, NAEP, TIMSS, and PISA, other state-mandated tests suggest that students are not performing as well as they should be. These tests are regularly taken at face value and used as justification for the rhetoric of failing schools. However, experts in education and psychological measurement are in virtually unanimous agreement that most state-mandated tests are poor measurement instruments that fail to capture growth, especially in low-income schools (see, for example, Downey, von Hipple, & Hughes, 2008). However, it is still extremely common for people from all areas inside and outside of education to suggest that teachers and schools are failing or that American schools don't stack up to schools in other countries. The narrative of failure proceeds without a meaningful discussion of what the functions of public schools are in society, and it is often based on claims that are not supported by valid, reliable evidence.

Often considered to be triggered by the publication of the book *A Nation at Risk* (National Commission on Excellence in Education, 1983), the narrative about an education system in crisis has been constructed and used to justify educational change (Berliner & Biddle, 1995). The subsequent efforts to manage this crisis have included political benefits to those who are best able to capitalize on the fear it engenders, as well as financial profit for those who offer privatized alternatives (Glass, 2008; Smith, 2004). In line with a multiple streams framework (Zahariadis, 2007), the crisis of educational failure can be understood as simply a convenient policy window to enact a solution that had preceded any real problem. The desire for power prompted the search for evidence of failure. Although the prevalence of crisis rhetoric and its detachment from the real achievements of public schools has been well documented, the narrative still has a strong hold on people's conceptions of education and detracts from critical thinking about the role that public education plays in the lives of American children and what the true functions of a public education are in a democratic society.

The functions of public schools and how they reproduce the social structure of a society have been widely examined by educational sociologists and scholars (Bowles & Gintis, 2002; Coleman, 1987; Dreeben, 1967; Durkheim, 1961). Public schools have traditionally been defined as a socially reproductive mechanism that allows for the maintenance of a labor force. An ordered labor force requires a place for children to go during the day so that people can go to work. Thus, at a fundamental level, schools provide child care for members of an organized society. Schools also help to reproduce the labor force. As social and technological progress continues and older workers retire, newly trained workers need to be ready to take their place and meet the demands of a changing world. Additionally, schools also aid the enculturation of behavioral norms and social values that prepare children to participate with agency and intention in the body politic. In order for democratic societies to function properly, citizens must be able and willing to participate in decision making and governance.

Although today one of the predominant criticisms of public schools is that they are not adequately preparing students for the world of work (National Research Council, 2005), the major criticism among classic social scientists of schools' instrumentality in maintaining a labor force is that schools reproduce social stratification and concretize children into their respective class standings by providing different types of education for the rich and the poor (Anyon, 1981; Althusser, 1971; Bourdieu, 1973; Freire, 1987; Giroux, 1983). The transmission of power, privileges, cultural and behavioral norms, values, morals, and a relevant knowledge base has been within the purview of public education since its inception, and how public education functions with regard to social stratification has been widely examined (see, for example, Anyon, 1981; Giroux, 1983). One of the most subtle but powerful early criticisms of public schools was that educational institutions are able to hide the socially reproductive nature of the system. One way that this sorting mechanism has been concealed is by framing schools as gateways to economic success and social mobility. Early educational sociologists argued that a dominant ideology, or a belief system that governs social movement, frames public schools as picturesque pathways to liberation and freedom. This meritocratic ideology has been theorized to conceal the socially reproductive nature of public schools (Bourdieu & Passeron, 1973). That is, if one truly believes that any student can achieve anything in any school with effort and hard work, then the onus for poverty and social immobility rests solely on the child. Because reality is detached from ideology, schools position children into respective class standings, and little social mobility actually occurs.

In order for this type of ideological framing to persist, public schools must be perceived as meritocratic (Althusser, 1971). That is, public education must be considered a human right of which everyone has equal opportunity to take advantage. In turn, those who do not take advantage of that right have squandered the opportunity and fall victim to social immobility and poverty. Within this framework, the rhetoric surrounding public education conceals the educational system as the central mechanism of social and cultural reproduction. Although many believe that the education system provides the opportunity to move up the social ladder, reproductive theorists believe the system inculcates socially stratified lessons that reproduce poverty. Giroux (1983) describes the function of schools as threefold. First, schools provide different classes and social groups with the lessons, knowledge, and skills they need to fulfill their respective, stratified roles in society. Second, schools reproduce and distribute culturally legitimate forms of knowledge, values, language, and style reflective of the dominant culture. Third, schools are part of a state apparatus that produces and legitimates the economic and ideological imperatives that feed the states' political power.

With regard to the transmission of knowledge, values, and skills, Jean Anyon (1981), in a widely cited study, theorized that social reproduction takes place in part through teachers' interactions with students and their approach to classroom teaching. In her qualitative examination of five economically distinct schools, she found that teachers in lower socio-economic schools engaged students in a much different manner than teachers in wealthy schools. In the working-class schools, teachers were procedurally oriented and espoused less-sophisticated epistemological beliefs. Teachers in these schools communicated to children that correct answers could be found in textbooks, rules were meant to be followed, and steps were often emphasized. In contrast, students in the more affluent schools were treated differently by their teachers. Students in these classrooms were given much more choice in their study, and they were encouraged to conduct experiments and seek out answers on their own. Rules were made by the teacher in collaboration with the students, and creative, expressive work was encouraged. In her work, Anyon suggested that the differences in these practices were representative of the hidden curriculum of work. These varying practices contribute to the process of social reproduction by emphasizing different cognitive, behavioral, and affective habits and frames of mind that yield different forms of cultural capital and preparation for the future.

Though studies offered by thinkers such as Anyon and Giroux can be viewed as early criticisms of public schools and teachers, more recent work has offered inquiry into the way in which ideological mechanisms and strategic framing of political issues obscure the creation of public policy, which in turn impedes public school functioning (see, for example, Lakoff, 2004). This is an important development because it represents a shift in blame from teachers to policy creation. This body of research has demonstrated the ways in which ideological belief systems lead to policy that benefits the well off and conceals the plight of the disenfranchised. For example, Berliner and Biddle (1995) took great pains to demonstrate the disconnect that exists between the rhetoric surrounding public schools and the functioning of the schools. By analyzing disaggregated criterion-referenced test data, these authors demonstrated that although public schools continue to help students make gains in nationally normed standardized tests such as the SAT, schools and teachers in the United States continue to be framed as "failing." Additionally, the rhetoric of failing schools has been used to advance the privatization movement and school vouchers initiatives (Smith, 2004), which many educational theorists believe may increase the already vast differences between the haves and have-nots.

Most important, however, and perhaps central to all of the work discussed above, is the notion that ideology lulls people into a state of continuous reform efforts and takes the focus off the real problems of child poverty we have in the United States by suggesting that if poor children and teachers in urban schools simply worked harder, then the achievement gap between the rich and the poor would close. Ideology distorts people's relationship with the actual state and functions of public schools by focusing on meritocratic myths, crisis, and failure. Ideological narratives about public schools suggest that with the right kind of effort, all students can achieve at any level regardless of their social class, leaving teachers and schools as the only logical barrier to success. Clearly the factors that impact social mobility in the United States are largely out of the control of public school teachers, and the notion that widespread social mobility is common in the United States is, in and of itself, a myth.

Poverty and the Functions of Public Schools

The myth of meritocracy is a powerful ideological apparatus that suggests that all students, no matter what their background, can achieve any goal with the right kind of effort. Based on the prevailing assumption that all people can simply pull themselves up by their bootstraps, and the ideological implication that schools impede this process, a couple of other objectives have emerged for public schools. These functions have emerged from the rhetoric of meritocracy and the intense focus on the unacceptable conditions of many public schools in lower socio-economic environments that serve underrepresented minority groups.

Schools are rhetorically framed as responsible for closing the achievement gap between racial groups in the United States (Kober, 2001). Data consistently show an achievement gap among Whites, Asians, Blacks, and Hispanics on standardized test scores, with Blacks and Hispanics scoring lower than Whites and Asians. In a similar vein, maintaining international competitiveness on standardized tests (National Commission on Excellence in Education, 1983; National Research Council, 2005) has also been added to the list of public school functions. Schools are commonly described as failing to adequately educate American students to compete with their counterparts in other countries on internationally norm-referenced tests, especially in math and science.

These two functions emerged after the Civil Rights Movement and toward the end of the Cold War, respectively. The addition of these functions complicated our vision of excellence and increased debate about where, how, and why we need to improve. Our desire to close the achievement gap has exposed systemic inequalities in the fabric of our economy, and our increased focus on competition, both within and between borders, has led to forced allegiance from teachers and schools to problematic educational policy. Policymakers almost universally conclude that we have failed to meet our goals, and that poor teaching, low expectations, poor curriculum, undisciplined school climates, and the like are to blame for these perceived failures of public schools (Rothstein, 2004). The implicit assumptions underlying this thinking are that it is the schools' fault that inequalities in academic achievement exist and that schools can fix these inequalities when the right kind of teaching and instruction are provided.

There are fundamental problems with these assumptions, primarily rooted in the fact that while the American Dream can come true for individuals, it does not come true for populations. The United States has the second-highest rate of child poverty and the most persistent rate of poverty of any other Western industrialized country (Berliner, 2006). The sheer number of children who suffer from poverty in the United States reflects our achievement gap. By and large, students in poorer schools perform less well than students in wealthier schools (Berliner, 2006; Rothstein, 2004). By and large, poorer people in the United States are Black and Hispanic. So, when politicians and educators talk about closing the achievement gap, they are really talking about making sweeping changes in educational achievement at the national level in a country with the highest rates of poverty of any Western industrialized country. Obviously, this goal takes more than dramatic educational reform. Yet the prevalent ideology that surrounds public schools is that with the right kind of effort, all students can succeed regardless of their social class. This ideology blatantly ignores and trivializes the restrictive nature of poverty. Again, social change may be possible at the individual level, but it is not coming to pass for the general population in the United States. This is an important distinction, because most educational policy is based on a message of failure about what *can* be true for individuals, not what *is* true for populations.

Teachers' Perceptions of the Functions of Public Schools

Paradoxically, the same ideology that has come to dominate problematic and damaging educational policies may be the same ideology that motivates many educators to enter the profession and work hard at being quality educators. Thus, it is possible that working to undo the ideological message of failure that is damaging on a macro level might undo what can be considered an effective meta-strategy for increasing and maintaining people's optimism about teaching. That is, the ideological conception that all students, no matter where they are from, can achieve anything they want with the right type of motivation, drive, and effort could be considered an adaptive ideology for teachers in that attributionally there is hope for a bright future for all students. In a sense, the flip side of this ideology, or focusing on how social ills such as poverty and deteriorating communities influence education, rather than the other way around, is the fatal flaw of an educator and extinguishes the all-important passion and commitment exemplary of quality teaching.

However, at a macro level, this type of ideology is detrimental because, from a policy perspective, it shifts the blame for economic disparity from those who regulate the economic structures in the United States to teachers and schools. Americans have seen how the burdens of economic failure in the United States can be shifted from those who caused them to those who suffered from them, and the case of education is no different. If any student can achieve any goal with motivation and effort, then the easy, jump-to-the-wrong-conclusion solution is that children remain in poverty because teachers and students are not fulfilling their potential. The burden is shifted from the causes of the problem (that is, historical oppression, deleterious child poverty, and inattention to quality health and child care) to those who suffer from them.

It is also difficult to explain to teachers that an unwavering belief in the ability of all children to achieve is the rationale for damaging educational policy and an excuse to allow poverty to persist in the United States without meaningful intervention (Gerstl-Pepin, 2006). Although research can illuminate the problems faced by children in poverty and highlight the impact of our current economic structure on educational attainment, it can also illuminate problems that are hard for teachers to face. When considering the number of children in the United States who live below the poverty line and the horrible conditions many of them face, teachers may shift their incremental attributions of success to entity-driven stereotypes of poverty and learned helplessness—an even worse cultural deficit model.

The paradox here is crystal clear: the ideology of control that works to shift blame for the manufactured educational crisis in the United States from economic conditions and deteriorating communities to hardworking teachers and schools is the same ideology that drives many educators to be agents of change. Undoing the macro version of this form of ideological control while keeping incremental attributions about children intact is the careful realm of teacher educators who want to unveil damaging educational policy and beliefs about the role of education in a democratic society but do not want to dissuade hardworking and well-intentioned teachers from staying in the field of education.

Although the prevailing meritocratic ideology leads to damaging policy, the public schools and the teachers in them who espouse similar beliefs do not cause harm. This combination makes for a resistant strain of ideology that is difficult to decipher and combat. Schools are the sites where most of the transformation and change take place, which are immense, considering the consistent educational progress over the years. This change takes place because of the unwavering teacher belief that students are capable of anything they put their minds to. But the policy that stems from the same belief system has led to ineffective reforms. If teachers have been able to help students to progress consistently over the years, how much have reforms such as increased accountability, testing, and so-called school choice impacted positive change in either achievement or social mobility? As it turns out, much of the best research in education suggests that these approaches actually do little to help students achieve and may actually increase the achievement gap and limit effective teaching (Molnar, 2002).

Misconceptions about Public School Functioning

The dominant narrative about American education is that teachers and schools have failed to adequately educate a lazy American populace. Yet we have seen that the evidence showing how teachers and schools have failed is often ideological, perfunctory, doctored, or invalid and unreliable. It is common for the media to report that American students do not perform well in math and science compared to students from other countries, do not perform well on state standardized tests, or are not being adequately prepared for the world of work. Time and again, however, thoughtful researchers have shown empirical evidence that few if any of these accusations are completely correct.

Examination of disaggregated international test scores suggests that students from the middle and upper classes in the United States rank in the top three in all academic categories: math, science, and reading (Lemke et al., 2001). Moreover, research suggests that SAT, NAEP, and IQ test scores have been on the rise for decades, with the greatest increases among marginalized populations who have had to overcome hundreds of years of oppression in and out of school (Bracey, 2003). These successes have been realized in the face of extreme adversity. Although civil rights progress has been made and historically oppressed groups have made the most gains in recent decades on standardized tests (Berliner, 2006; Berliner & Biddle, 1995; Bracey, 2003, Glass, 2008), U.S. schools are now more segregated than they were before *Brown v. Board of Education* (Kozol, 2005), and the United States ranks last among Western industrialized countries in child poverty rates (Berliner, 2006). Roughly one in four children in the United States lives below the poverty line, and the rate of child poverty in America has been steadily rising since 1980, while the concentration of wealth has siphoned to the top 1% in the country (United for a Fair Economy, 2009; U.S. Census Bureau Summary, 2003).

Despite these profound problems in our economic and social structures, teachers continue to produce rather amazing results. Although barriers to success for children in our country mount steadily as our economic and social infrastructures deteriorate, teachers continue to help students make steady progress. The prevailing misconception, however, is that the quality of education in the United States is decreasing. The reality is that the quality of life in the United States has been decreasing, which in turn negatively impacts education. The narrative of failure that underlies these misconceptions is difficult to decipher, and teachers have been forced to abide by related policies and—probably to some degree—swindled into agreeing with their philosophical underpinnings. It is hard for anyone to argue against improving schools. Yet forcing allegiance through the rhetoric of chaos and the need for change (Glass, 2008) and using crises as the rationale for policy change and political power (Berliner & Biddle, 1995) have not improved public education. At face value, these policies promise increased equity, social mobility, and access, yet their actual impact has been increased school segregation, higher dropout rates, and a movement toward privatized education that will probably not help to meet our educational goals.

Many well-intentioned people believe that we have failed to meet our educational goals because teachers and schools have failed. Good intentions, in this case, are misleading, and policymakers have placed increasing amounts of blame on public schools and teachers, which has overshadowed the economic and social causes for the pockets of struggling students we have in the United States (Rothstein, 2004). Fuchs (2002) makes a similar argument with regard to health care. He argues that, from a population perspective, access to health care (although important) is not nearly as significant as environmental factors and personal behavioral choices in impacting measurable health outcomes. Changes in these factors are reflected in the health care institution but are not attributable to it. Changes in student achievement and school functioning at the population level are largely due to changes in environmental factors, living conditions, and personal choices, and are not attributable to educational institutions. This is not to say that schools cannot and do not make an impact, but rather that meeting educational goals such as closing the achievement gap requires improving the quality of life for children. Only by acknowledging this side of the equation can true change be recognized.

Consider this analogy: When illness is on the rise, people don't merely blame doctors and hospitals for causing the illness. Doctors and researchers attempt to examine the illness more carefully and target systemic causes that are generally due to environmental or genetic factors. Yet when learning difficulties are on the rise, we have a bad habit of merely blaming teachers and schools and not accounting for external factors. What common sense *should* be telling us is that we need to examine learning a little more closely and target systemic causes of academic difficulty such as poverty and its related issues: food insecurity, joblessness, segregated housing, lack of adequate child care, and school overcrowding (Berliner, 2006; Glass, 2008; Rothstein, 2008). We should recognize that teachers and schools are part of the solution, not the problem, and focus on reform measures that have demonstrated the most empirical evidence for positive change, especially within pockets of struggling students.

However, the widespread ideological misconceptions about public schools have led to policies at both state and federal levels that promote increased school accountability, standardization, and competition to promote educational change (Glass, 2008; Hursh, 2007a). Many policymakers purport that increased school accountability, high-stakes testing, and school competition can help us achieve our educational goals of maintaining a labor force, closing the achievement gap, and improving international standings. However, evidence suggests that these approaches have led to a number of detrimental side effects (Amrein & Berliner, 2002; Au, 2007; Bracey, 2006; Darling-Hammond, 2007; Harris & Herrington, 2006; Hursh, 2007b; Nichols & Berliner, 2006), not limited to an increased achievement gap and tailorized curriculums that ignore the whole child. In particular, a myopic focus on testing and accountability (Kober, 2001; Orfield & Lee, 2005), systemic problems with the way achievement is measured (Downey, von Hipple, & Hughes, 2008; Lee, 2002), spurious conclusions about education and the free market (Glass, 2008; Smith, 2004), and obfuscation of the differences between individuals and populations have actually moved us further away from our desired goals.

Unfortunately, it has become difficult to discuss school reform or even school improvement without invoking the rhetoric of failing schools. Wanting to improve instructional methods or children's education is not synonymous with the notion that schools are failing, although the two are undoubtedly conflated, especially in the political realm. Ironically enough, the school reform proposals that have shown the best empirical evidence of success are those that are not tied to the rhetoric of school failure and can be implemented, by and large, without dramatic changes. They do not rely on the privatization of education, the implementation of charter schools, or school competition. Although charter schools, school vouchers, and other dramatic methods of reform have shown little to no evidence of success (Berliner, 2006; Bracey, 2003; Glass, 2008), research into high-quality early childhood education, class size reduction in grades K–3, and teacher practices has produced evidence that changes in these areas can yield substantial student improvements, especially in economically depressed areas where help is needed. High-quality early childhood programs focused on disadvantaged children (Barrett, 2002; Campbell & Ramey, 1999; Schweinhart, 2004), highly qualified certified teachers who employ effective teaching methods and logical consequences (Darling-Hammond, 2000; Glass, 2002; Haberman, 1995), and small teacher-to-student ratios in the early grades (Achilles, 1999; Ehrenberg, 2001; Finn, 2002; Glass & Smith, 1978) have all been shown to produce the largest positive effects on student achievement.

Additionally, changes in the economic conditions of depressed areas, or improving the quality of life of those suffering from poverty, have also been shown to improve student academic achievement. Reframing educational reform to include community improvement and reducing economic stratification is an important idea in educational policy (Anyon & Greene, 2007; Berliner, 2006), and a handful of studies have shown that areas that undergo sustained economic improvement tend to experience large educational gains among students in subsequent generations (Dearing, McCartney, & Taylor, 2001; Taylor, Dearing, & McCartney, 2004). Empirical research tells us that students who are provided with meaningful educational experiences from an early age, who spend more time engaged in thoughtful interactions with well-prepared teachers, and who are allowed the opportunity to learn in small classes where they receive lots of feedback during instruction tend to achieve at much higher rates. Research also tells us that increased competition in the classroom, high-stakes standardized testing, charter schools, and privatization efforts have shown little to no evidence of improving student performance beyond that of public schools and, in the case of some of these efforts, have actually been shown to increase dropout rates and decrease student performance, especially in areas where help is needed (Amrein & Berliner, 2002; Au, 2007; Bracey, 2006; Darling-Hammond, 2007; Harris & Herrington, 2006; Nichols & Berliner, 2006). It should probably not be a surprise, however, that the empty rhetoric of failing schools is attached to empty school reform proposals.

If what we really want for our nation is to maintain an effective labor force, close the achievement gap between ethnic groups, and improve our international standing in education, then we should be doing what the research tells us will work. If we want these things, we need to improve access to high-quality child care, reduce class sizes, produce well-prepared certified teachers, and improve the economic conditions for the poor in our country.

Evidence suggests that these approaches will work, especially when targeted at economically disadvantaged areas. Unfortunately, these pragmatic and logical approaches to school reform have not gained ground in recent years and have lost out to unproven approaches linked to problematic ideology.

Charter schools, privatization efforts, and increased testing and accountability measures also yield profits for entrepreneurs and corporations, whereas class size reduction, improved teacher preparation, increased access to high-quality early child care, and increased prosperity for the poor, at first glance, presumably do not. However, cost-benefit analyses of these types of interventions suggest that these measures save money in other ways. For example, studies show that for every $1 invested in high-quality early education in disadvantaged areas, $3 to $12 can be saved in the long run on expenses such as special education, the criminal justice system, and the prison system (Reynolds, Temple, Robertson, & Mann, 2001; Schweinhart, 2004). Savings through prevention of future problems are everywhere in education.

If our educational goals for this nation are to transition public education into a post-democratic world where the risk of being uneducated is distributed among children, and our vulnerabilities are shrouded in ideology that benefits the strong, then our current ideology and approach to reform is appropriate and effective. If our educational goals for this nation are to maintain an effective labor force, close the achievement gap, and improve our international standing in education, then we need to implement lasting research-based practices that have been shown to result in meaningful improvements for our nation's children. This includes starting to consider public schools as part of the solution rather than part of the problem.

References

Achilles, C.M. (1999). *Let's put kids first finally: Getting class size right.* Thousand Oaks, CA: Corwin Press.

Althusser, L. (1971). *Lenin and philosophy, and other essays.* London: New Left Books.

Amrein, A.L., & Berliner, D.C. (2002). High-stakes testing, uncertainty, and student learning. *Education Policy Analysis Archives, 10*(18). Retrieved February 2, 2010, from http://epaa.asu.edu/epaa/v10n18/

Anyon, J. (1981). Social class and school knowledge. *Curriculum Inquiry, 11*, 3–42.

Anyon, J., & Greene, K. (2007). No Child Left Behind as an anti-poverty measure. *Teacher Education Quarterly, 34*(2), 157–162.

Au, W. (2007). High-stakes testing and curricular control: A qualitative metasynthesis. *Educational Researcher, 36*(5), 258–267.

Barrett, W.S. (2002). Early childhood education. In A. Molnar (Ed.), *School reform proposals: The research evidence* (pp. 1–26). Greenwich, CT: Information Age Publishing.

Berliner, D.C. (2006). Our impoverished view of education research. *Teachers College Record, 108*(6), 949–995.

Berliner, D.C., & Biddle, B.J. (1995). *The manufactured crisis: Myths, fraud, and the attack on America's public schools.* New York: HarperCollins.

Bourdieu, P. (1973). Cultural reproduction and social reproduction. In R. Brown (Ed.), *Knowledge, education, and cultural change* (pp. 71–112). London: Tavistock.

Bourdieu, P., & Passeron, J.C. (1973). *Cultural reproduction in education society and culture.* Thousand Oaks, CA: Sage.

Bowles, S., & Gintis, H. (2002). Schooling in capitalist America revisited. *Sociology of Education, 75*, 1–18.

Bracey, G. (2003). Those misleading SAT and NAEP trends: Simpson's paradox at work. *Education Disinformation Detection and Reporting Agency.* Retrieved May 2010 from http://www.america-tomorrow.com/bracey/EDDRA/EDDRA30.htm

———. (2006, October). The 16th Bracey report on the condition of public education. *Phi Delta Kappan*, pp. 151–166.

Campbell, F., & Ramey, C. (1999). *Early learning, later success: The Abecedarian study early childhood educational intervention for poor children: The executive summary.* Retrieved May 2010 from http://www.fpg.unc.edu/~abc/ells-04.pdf

Coleman, J. (1987). Relations between schools and social structure. In M.T. Hallinan (Ed.), *The social organization of schools* (pp. 177–204). New York: Plenum Press.

Darling-Hammond, L. (2000). Teacher quality and student achievement: A review of state policy evidence. *Education Policy Analysis Archives, 8*(1). Available at http://epaa.asu.edu/epaa/v8n1

———. (2007). Race, inequality and accountability: The irony of No Child Left Behind. *Race Ethnicity and Education, 10*(3), 245–260.

Dearing, E., McCartney, K., & Taylor, B.A. (2001). Change in family income-to-needs matters more for children with less. *Child Development, 72*(6), 1779–1793.

Downey, D.B., von Hipple, P.T., & Hughes, M. (2008). Are "failing" schools really failing? Using seasonal comparison to evaluate school effectiveness. *Sociology of Education, 81*, 242–270.

Dreeben, R. (1967). The contribution of schooling to the learning of norms. *Harvard Educational Review, 57*, 211–237.

Durkheim, E. (1961). *Moral education.* New York: The Free Press.

Ehrenberg, R.G. (2001). Class size and student achievement. *Psychological Science in the Public Interest, 1*(1), 1-30.

Finn, J.D. (2002). Class-size reduction in grades K–3. In A. Molnar (Ed.), *School reform proposals: The research evidence* (pp. 27–48). Greenwich, CT: Information Age.

Flynn, J.R. (1994). IQ gains over time. In R.J. Sternberg (Ed.), *Encyclopedia of human intelligence* (pp. 617–623). New York: Macmillan.

Freire, P. (1987). *Pedagogy of the oppressed* (M. Bergman Ramos, Trans.). New York: Continuum.

Fuchs, V. (2002). *Who shall live: Health, economics and social choice.* River Ridge, NJ: Word Scientific.

Gerstl-Pepin, C.I. (2006). The paradox of poverty narrative: Educators struggling with children left behind. *Educational Policy, 20*(1), 143–162.

Giroux, H.A. (1983). Theories of reproduction and resistance in the new sociology of education: A critical analysis. *Harvard Educational Review, 53*, 257–293.

Glass, G.V. (2002). Teacher characteristics. In A. Molnar (Ed.), *School reform proposals: The research evidence* (pp. 155–174). Greenwich, CT: Information Age.

———. (2008). *Fertilizers, pills, and magnetic strips: The fate of public education in America.* New York: Information Age.

Glass, G.V., & Smith, M.L. (1978). *Meta-analysis of research on the relationship of class size and achievement.* San Francisco, CA: Far West Laboratory for Educational Research and Development.

Haberman, M. (1995). *Star teachers of children in poverty.* Bloomington, IN: Kappa Delta Phi.

Harris, D.N., & Herrington, C.D. (2006). Accountability, standards, and the growing achievement gap: Lessons from the past half-century. *American Journal of Education, 112*, 209–238.

Hursh, D. (2007a). Assessing No Child Left Behind and the rise of neoliberal education policies. *American Educational Research Journal, 44*(3), 493–518.

———. (2007b). Exacerbating inequality: The failed promise of the No Child Left Behind Act. *Race Ethnicity and Education, 10*(3), 295–308.

Kober, N. (2001). *It takes more than testing: Closing the achievement gap.* A report of the Center on Educational Policy. Cleveland, OH: George Gund Foundation.

Kozol, J. (2005). *The shame of the nation: The restoration of apartheid schooling in America.* New York: Three Rivers Press.

Lakoff, G. (2004). *Don't think of an elephant: Know your values and frame the debate.* White River Junction, VT: Chelsea Green Publishing.

Lee, J. (2002). Racial and ethnic achievement gap trends: Reversing the progress toward equity? *Educational Researcher*, *31*(1), 3–12.

Lemke, M., Calsyn, C., Lippman, L., Jocelyn, L., Kastberg, D., Liu, Y.Y, Roey, S., Williams, T., Kruger, T., & Bairu, G. (2001). *Outcomes of learning: Results from the 2000 program for international student assessment of 15-year-olds in reading, mathematics, and science literacy* (NCES 2002-115). Washington, DC: U.S. Department of Education, National Center for Education Statistics.

Molnar, A. (Ed.). (2002). *School reform proposals: The research evidence.* Greenwich, CT: Information Age.

National Commission on Excellence in Education. (1983). *A nation at risk: A report to the nation and the secretary of education.* Washington, DC: U.S. Department of Education.

National Research Council. (2005). *Rising above the gathering storm: Energizing and employing America for a brighter economic future.* Committee on Prospering in the Global Economy of the 21st Century: An Agenda for American Science and Technology, National Academy of Sciences, National Academy of Engineering, Institute of Medicine.

Nichols, S.N., & Berliner, D.C. (2006). *The inevitable corruption of indicators and educators through high-stakes testing.* Tempe, AZ: College of Education, Education Policy Studies (Laboratory Report EPSL 0503-101-EPRU). Retrieved May 2010 from http://epsl.asu.edu/high-stakes-testing.htm

Orfield, G., & Lee, C. (2005). *Why segregation matters: Poverty and educational inequality.* Cambridge, MA: The Civil Rights Project, Harvard University.

Phi Delta Kappa/Gallup Poll. (2001, May 23–June 6). Retrieved May 2010 from http://www.pdkintl.org./kappan/k0109gal.htm

Reynolds, A.J., Temple, J.A., Robertson, D.L., & Mann, E.A. (2001). Age 21 cost-benefit analysis of the Title I Chicago Child-Parent Center Program Executive Summary. Retrieved May 2010 from http://www.waisman.wisc.edu/cls/cbaexecsum4.html

Rothstein, R. (2004). *Class and schools: Using social, economic, and educational reform to close the black-white achievement gap.* Washington, DC: Economic Policy Institute.

———. (2008). Whose problem is poverty? *Educational Leadership*, *65*(7), 8–13.

Schweinhart, L.J. (2004). *The HighScope Perry Preschool Study through age 40: Summary, conclusions, and frequently asked questions.* Ypsilanti, MI: HighScope Press.

Smith, M.L. (2004). *Political spectacle and the fate of American schools.* New York: Taylor & Francis.

Taylor, B.A., Dearing, E., & McCartney K. (2004). Incomes and outcomes in early childhood. *Journal of Human Resources*, *39*(4), 980–1007.

United for a Fair Economy. (2009). *The growing divide*. Retrieved May 2010 from http://www.faireconomy.org/issues/growing_divide

U.S. Census Bureau Summary. (2003). *Income, poverty, and health insurance coverage in the United States*. Retrieved May 2010 from http://www.census.gov/prod/2004pubs/p60-226.pdf

Zahariadis, N. (2007). The multiple streams framework: Structure, limitations, prospects. In P. A. Sabatier (Ed.), *Theories of policy process* (2nd ed., pp. 65–92). Cambridge, MA: Westview Press.

❖ CHAPTER FOUR ❖

Obama's Educational Policy: Disposition of Authenticity or the Politics of *The Emperor's New Clothes*

Stella C. Batagiannis

With the campaign and election of Barack Obama as President of the United States of America came a sorely needed resurgence of hope in our country, one we had not seen in decades—perhaps not since the days of the Kennedys and their Camelot and the idealism of the 1960s. That hope was founded on an expectation that Obama possessed the disposition of authenticity and that it would result in actions reflective of that disposition.

Like so many Americans, I, too, felt that hope again—and in some ways, perhaps, more deeply—as an immigrant whose parents came to the United States to pursue the American Dream. Our parents brought my brother and me to Gary, Indiana, when we were ages 9 and 7, respectively. Our mother and father left their native country, Greece, when they were in their late 30s. It took great courage to leave behind family, friends, and their language to come to a country they had never even visited and with two young children in tow. To add to that hardship, our father was separated from us for 3 years until the immigration lines reopened and we could join him. I am often asked why our parents made that decision. The answer is simple and, to me, obvious: they wanted to pursue the American Dream for themselves and, especially, for my brother and me.

And for me the American Dream has been all about commitment to education, always fueled by passion about effecting change in students' lives and making a difference in our society. Since the age of 7, I knew I wanted to teach. Indeed, I have spent my entire professional life in education, first teaching high school English, then serving as a principal and a superintendent, and now teaching future principals as a university professor. In the past year, the hope that Obama's campaign and election generated has been quickly dissipating for educators (Dionne, 2010; Giroux, 2009; Ravitch,

2010). And it is my own personal history that causes me to feel the disappointment differently, at least, if not more poignantly, as we watch our nation and the American Dream threatened by policymakers who dismiss deep learning in education, exhibit neither vision nor even common sense, and often engage in the singular pursuit of money and power. Contrary to what policymakers claim, it is not public education that is endangering our nation, but their own foolish and simplistic notions (at best) and greedy, divisive tactics (at worst): in other words, political decisions reflecting the absence of the disposition of authenticity.

One of the areas on which these policymakers have focused is that of deciding who should teach and who should lead schools. The lack of respect for education (Bracey, 2002; Giroux, 2009; Kozol, 2005a, 2005b) is reflected in their idea that anyone—any businessman, for example—can walk in and teach or be a principal or superintendent. However, only school leadership that understands the complexities of education (Foster, 1986; Fullan, 2005; Hargreaves & Fink, 2006; Heifetz, 1994; Kanpol & Yeo, 2000; Winchester, 2007) will succeed. Personally, I chose to move through each of the leadership chairs so that I would have a better understanding of educational leadership. And each step was invaluable in gaining deeper insight, which, in turn, inspired creative ideas such as an alternative school founded on the ethic of care and student leadership, a Teacher-on-Special-Assignment initiative to include the voice of teachers in curriculum leadership, and an Education Foundation to draw in community and to support teacher creativity and innovation through small grants. Most of my colleagues have similarly chosen to move through each of the leadership positions. How lacking in common sense that one who has never been in a classroom is now going to lead a school or district or even all schools in the nation—and how indicative of the lack of respect for educators, mentioned above, that seems to permeate our society.

But in these tumultuous times for education, policymakers continue to move to dismantle public education, to insist on instantaneous perfection[2] (Batagiannis, 2007), to push for privatization, and to focus on high-stakes testing and narrow standards (Bracey, 2002; Ravitch 2009b, 2010). In the cacophony of policymakers' attacks and these demands for quick, superficial, and misnamed "reform," the deeper issue is often overlooked of who is qualified to work with children in the classroom, to lead a school, or to provide leadership as Secretary of Education or President of the United States. And that deeper issue consists of the dispositions that leaders possess or lack.

In examining the dispositions of President Barack Obama, I focus in this chapter on the disposition of authenticity. Integral to this disposition are honesty and integrity, the valuing of public education, commitment to a democratic community, and policies and practices consistent with authenticity. This disposition seems to be the fount of the powerful hope of those who elected Obama. Its absence, however, is the source of equally strong frustration for some of these same constituents, including the educators who now observe his actions, which seem in direct contradiction to his words. If the rhetoric is only that and nothing more, Obama will be one more typical, albeit very articulate, politician. If his dispositions are instead authentically reflected in both his words and his political actions, the promise of hope may be fulfilled. However, President Obama will have to act differently than what we have observed to this point in his presidency, and time is critical if he is to stem the dismantling of public education.

In this chapter, I (a) discuss the importance of dispositions in leadership, all necessarily founded on courage; (b) analyze the disposition of authenticity of President Barack Obama as reflected in his words and his actions; (c) analyze contradictions to Obama's disposition of authenticity in his words and his policy: deep versus technical issues in education, education as a private or public good, individualism and politics or community, and the ultimate contradiction—his choice of Secretary of Education Arne Duncan; and (d) conclude with a section entitled "Which Road Will President Obama Choose: Descent into Cynicism or Reigniting of Hope?" which illuminates the need for congruence between the disposition of authenticity and leadership actions if President Obama is, in fact, to reignite the hope for education and our nation that he promised as a candidate.

Dispositions Defined

Dispositions are not easily defined (Bogen, 2007; National Council for Accreditation of Teacher Education, 2006a, 2007; Turkmen, 2009), but they are critical to leadership nonetheless. Ritchhart and Perkins (2008) stressed that "Good thinking is not only a matter of skills, but also a matter of dispositions" (p. 58). Sockett (2009) defined dispositions as: "the property of the agent, manifest only in intentional action, and [functioning] as predictions about human actions" (p. 292). Perkins (1995) termed dispositions, "The proclivities that lead us in one direction rather than another within the freedom of action that we have" (p. 275) and even "The soul of intelligence, without which the understanding and know-how do little good" (p. 278). The Council of Chief State School Officers (1996) emphasized that "Knowledge, dispositions, and performances—belong together" (p. 8). Usher, Usher, and Usher (2003) concluded about teachers (and, I contend, this applies to school leaders as well):

> To understand the dynamics of teacher behavior and its effectiveness we must direct our attention to the nature of the practitioner's personal meanings or dispositions. ("Teacher Dispositions," para 1)

NCATE[3] (2006b) defined dispositions as:

> The values, commitments, and professional ethics that influence behaviors toward students, families, colleagues, and communities and affect student learning, motivation, and development as well as the educator's own professional growth. (p. 53)

As critical as these definitions all deem dispositions to be, it would seem that dispositions would not be an issue of debate and contention, but this is not so. Dispositions in education have been the subject of debate since being formally implemented in the field: INTASC[4] in 1992, ISLLC Standards[5] in 1996, and NCATE in 2002. As states began to include dispositions for teacher licensure, objections arose and debates began (Bogen, 2007). NCATE backed down from the debates and objections, particularly about social justice, and diluted the definition in 2007 (NCATE, 2007). The ISLLC Standards for educational leaders, adopted in 1996, initially showed insight in including dispositions in thc cxpcctations for school leaders (Council of Chief State School Officers, 1996). However, in 2008, the dispositions were excluded in the revision of the ISLLC Standards (Council of Chief State School Officers, 2008). The elimination of dispositions was purported to be the result of "simplification," but the focus, both overt and covert, was clearly now on policy—and narrow policy at that, not the practice of leadership. The omission of the dispositions reflected, in part, the current trend of policymakers to usurp the role of educational leaders almost entirely and to substitute technicians for leaders, assessed only by easily quantifiable standards.

With all this in mind, I contend that the insistence on recognizing the importance of dispositions only if they can be identified precisely and measured in quantitative terms focuses on the intellect alone and contradicts the very essence of dispositions. Dispositions are founded not on Likert scales and other quantitative measures, but on who we are as educators, leaders, and human beings deep in our hearts. Human beings have minds and intellect to be developed. But they also have hearts—and the emotions and needs that accompany them (Noddings, 1984; Ringe, 1950), which ultimately create the foundation for the intellect and deep learning. I move next to the definition of the disposition of authenticity, including the implications of inauthenticity. These concepts are the focus of the remainder of this chapter.

Disposition of Authenticity Defined

Underlying all leadership, including that of President Obama, courage, which I discussed in earlier work (Batagiannis, 2007), is requisite. Without courage, one can manage, but one cannot lead at any level. The disposition of authenticity and courage are also inextricably linked, as courage is the very foundation of each of the dispositions.

The origin of authenticity is the Greek, *authentikos*, meaning *genuine* (*Compact Oxford English Dictionary*, n.d.). The disposition of authenticity is defined by Vannini (2006) as the "properties of genuineness, realness…pragmatic, social, psychological experience of feeling *true to one's self*" (p. 236). He concluded that this sense of self and actions are intertwined: "We should believe that the meanings that an individual has associated with his/her sense of self will significantly shape his or her action, and the meanings associated with action will shape the sense of self" (p. 237). Nixon (2004) defined authenticity as the "public face of truthfulness and respect" (p. 250). In his book *The Audacity of Hope* (2006), Obama himself speaks of how we crave authenticity: "[W]e long for that most elusive quality in our leaders—the quality of authenticity, of being who you say you are, of possessing a truthfulness that goes beyond words" (pp. 79–80).

Authenticity requires honesty about issues, rather than hiding behind unsubstantiated claims, dishonest use of language, blame, and politics, which unfortunately has become today's norm. Our world has evolved into a global society and economy. All entities, including education, need to evolve as well. Sagor (2005) reminded us that perfection has not been attained at any time in history and is not likely to be reached by schools today. However, perfection, even instantaneous perfection, although not possible, is nonetheless being demanded. The graduation rate is a perfect example of such inauthenticity in the demands of policymakers. In the Industrial Age, society expected and demanded a different goal when it came to the high school graduation rate. At that time, society wanted a workforce to man the factories, and therefore policymakers and business owners did not want all children to pursue postsecondary education. Now, the expectation has changed as those jobs have disappeared—some because those industries no longer exist and some because business found it more profitable to take the jobs overseas. With the changes accompanying globalization, policymakers now demand instant, perfect results and a 100% graduation rate. They label anything less a failure of schools.

No Child Left Behind (NCLB), too, has heaped blame (Kozol, 2005a; Ohanian, 1999) and demands for instantaneous perfection (Batagiannis, 2007) on educators and is yet another example of inauthenticity. The title of the legislation is a powerful euphemism, but the substance of the legislation stands in stark contrast. Kozol (2005a) strongly criticizes NCLB for its attacks on educators: "[NCLB] is basically driven by the concept that teachers have an inherently perverse attraction to mediocrity, that we entered this career because we just love mediocrity, and only if we're scared out of our wits will we aspire to excellence" (p. 33). Even Diane Ravitch (2009a, 2009b, 2010), after initially supporting NCLB and serving as Assistant Secretary of Education under the first Bush administration in the 1990s, has now rendered a harsh yet candid critique of NCLB (Merrow, 2009). Ravitch stated:

> We know from the National Assessment of Educational Progress that actual improvement has been less in these past seven years than in the years preceding the passage of NCLB. In the meantime, schools have become test-obsessed in a way that is not conducive to good education. (Merrow, "On Balance," para 2)

The only point I would disagree with Ravitch on is her statement that schools are "test-obsessed." It is actually policymakers who are so obsessed and threaten schools with their very existence if they resist or fail to comply. Reflective of the disposition of authenticity, Ravitch (2009b) also pointed out that NCLB demonstrated no substantive results but only a "rhetorical benefit" related to narrowing the achievement gap. In her best-selling book *The Death and Life of the Great American School System* (2010), Ravitch talked about her surprising change of heart about NCLB and explained her objection to seeing public education replaced by "something market-based" (p. 13).

As for President Obama's position on educational matters, he has contradicted himself time and again, suggesting inauthenticity. In the next section I will address Obama's authenticity or inauthenticity as reflected in policy contradictions, specifically as related to the following topics: deep versus technical issues in education, education as a private or public good, individualism and politics or community, and the ultimate contradiction in his policy: his choice of Secretary of Education Arne Duncan.

Obama's Dispositions and Policy: Articulated Authenticity versus Contradictory Action

In defining authenticity, Obama (2006), as discussed in the previous section, spoke candidly of the risk of inauthenticity among politicians: "There is a constant danger…that a politician may lose his moral bearings and find himself entirely steered by the winds of public opinion" (p. 79). In contrast, he cites the example of Senator Paul Simon, describing his authenticity in the eyes of the people: "that he lived out his values: that he was honest, and that he stood up for what he believed in, and perhaps most of all that he cared about them [his constituency]" (p. 80). And this authenticity, defined and analyzed by President Obama himself, is the very disposition that we continue to hope to see in him.

But the disposition of authenticity in the political scene requires a broader vision and a different culture than does the market mentality currently touted to be the answer to all issues—and seemingly supported by President Obama—at least in education. That market lens is entirely different from one of authenticity and is founded on contrasting dispositions. For example, the person who purports to be an educator, but whose only view concerning students is that of customer and business provider, can offer surface learning, but not authentic school reform. The changes this individual suggests will be narrow, at best, because his or her priorities are not founded on the powerful disposition of authenticity and what is morally necessary or educationally sound, but only on profit.

The lack of authenticity of policymakers immersed in the market mentality is affecting schools today. School leaders are now expected to listen to the last "best" solution of the policymaker who wields the most political power. Although policymakers profess to be research-based in educational decisions, too often that has come to mean applying that label when it is politically expedient to do so. Leaders are to accept these opinions, absent authenticity, as fact, even "research," and dutifully reject their own knowledge about children and learning gained over years of study and experience. This distasteful and disrespectful blend of inauthenticity and politics is quite reminiscent of the fairy tale we read as children, *The Emperor's New Clothes*. In that tale, people claimed to see the emperor parading down the street in his new finery, even as they watched him marching along in his underwear. The only ones who spoke the truth were the little children:

> "What handsome new clothes the emperor has! How beautifully they fit him!" Nobody would admit they saw nothing, because they were afraid to appear stupid.
> "But he hasn't got anything on!" cried a child....
> And the emperor walked on still more majestically, and his aides walked behind and carried his imaginary train, which didn't exist at all. (King, 1996, p. 15)

To reiterate, many policymakers lack the courage to be authentic and to lead by speaking the truth. In addition, they expect school leaders to be equally inauthentic by "seeing"—like the emperor's subjects—only what the policymakers define as "reform" or risk reprisals or the withdrawal of funding. For example, Indiana is preparing to retain third graders if they are not reading at grade level. This decision is contrary to the research on retention and contrary to recent, similar retention experiences, including in Chicago and New York (Goldberg, 2005). Yet policymakers are moving forward without thought or wisdom and expecting educators to be inauthentic by developing and implementing a plan they know is not educationally or morally sound. *Race to the Top* is another clear example of the latter. Last week a capable and reflective future principal whispered in my office her concern about just this issue and wondered out loud, although in hushed tones, whether her superintendent believed what he was forced to verbalize in order for his district to be considered for additional monies. Goodlad (2007) relates a similar experience with several principals: "They feel guilty in trying to defend the policies and practices they are called upon to support....They are torn between coming out into public discourse regarding their concerns on these difficult questions and supporting the district's need to comply with federal law. The dilemma keeps them awake at night" (p. 57).

And that is every educator's struggle today. Should he or she voice a position about learning and students based on education and experience, or should he or she instead remain silent and, thus, appear to agree with what the educator actually opposes in order to pursue the financial "carrot" proffered by policymakers? Our nation, founded on the right to free speech, has withdrawn that very right from educators responsible for educating the next generation of citizens. Not only are the voices of educators thus being silenced, but also so will be those of future citizens—today's children.

Giroux (2009) candidly challenged President Obama's authenticity by comparing Obama's actions related to education with those committed to the market and seeking to undermine public education:

> Regarding the purpose and meaning of education, Obama's views do not differ significantly from those of many conservatives who have attempted for the last thirty years to undermine public and higher education with market-driven rationalities. Obama consistently argues that the relevance of education lies primarily in creating a trained workforce that will enable the United States to compete in a competitive global economy. (p. 257)

Giroux then identified a list of issues Obama supports, reflecting an anti-public schools disposition:

> Obama's support for vouchers, charter schools, merit pay for teachers, the use of financial incentives to reward students, privatization, limiting the bargaining power of teacher unions, and high-stakes testing schemes appears incompatible with his post-partisan view of education. (p. 259)

Disappointingly, too, when President Obama visited a school in America's capital, he chose a charter school. Again, the message appears clear as to his dispositions related to public education and in contradiction to his words. Authenticity is not reflected in his actions, and words are not enough.

As for the narrow content insisted upon by policymakers, how did policymakers decide that students, and society generally, need an education that is comprised of narrow bits of information, reflective of the old Back to Basics movement? The latter elicited questions of merit even in the Industrial Age, and it is even more incongruous in the Information Age. This narrow, myopic view of education does not begin to reflect the breadth and depth of learning offered by the Information Age, which more than ever needs teachers who embody both the science and art of teaching. *Globalization*, a term on the lips of every policymaker, will not be served best by scripted teaching and unrelated pieces of information substituted for a cohesive curriculum founded on higher-order thinking skills. Interestingly and appropriately, Zhao (2009) wonders at the oddity of educational decisions being made in the United States that are contrary to what other countries, such as China, have observed in our educational system in the past and are now emulating: "But most vexing is why Americans, who hold individual rights and liberty in the highest regard, would allow the government to dictate what their children should learn, when they should learn it, and how they are evaluated?" (p. vii).

For years there has been an effort to privatize education, the last "billion-dollar industry" (Bracey, 2002), and now the proponents of privatization seem to have President Obama's support as reflected in his policy decisions. Obama has continued the dismantling of public education at an unexpected level that continues and exceeds the efforts of Bush in the previous 8 years (Ravitch, 2009b)—because Obama has now thrown money at his plan. By doing so at the same time that states are withdrawing financial support of public education, he is silencing the voices of educators as they are forced to seek *Race to the Top* funding. In other words, educators are forced to pursue money in return for being silent and/or even being part of the dismantling of public education, the move to privatization, and all that these two moves portend. With the dissolution of public education, as stated earlier, will come the further widening of the achievement gap and the further division of our country into the "haves" and the "have-nots," the "American apartheid," of which Kozol (2005a, 2005b) speaks. And those of us who elected Obama believe he should know better.

Public schools at the P–12 level and now higher education continue to be under attack. Merrow (2009) interviewed Ravitch, who quoted Mike Petrilli of the Fordham Institute, a conservative fortress: "If you found *No Child Left Behind* prescriptive, just wait till you take a look at this baby [*Race to the Top*]" (Petrilli, 2009). Even a year ago, some of my graduate students, as we read Bracey's (2002) *The War Against America's Public Schools*, argued naively that there was no political agenda against the public schools. This year, the same students are silent as they look on at the fast-moving, impending dismantling of public education.

Education seems to have always been the scapegoat in America. Berliner and Biddle (1995) speak of their "outrage" once they became aware of "powerful people…pursuing a political agenda designed to weaken the nation's public schools…[and] prepared to tell lies, suppress evidence, scapegoat educators, and sow endless confusion. We consider this conduct particularly despicable" (p. xii). Bracey (2002) also points to the blame that has consistently been heaped on schools for our society's problems: "Each time the United Sates faces a social crisis of some kind, the schools get blamed for it. They took the hit for letting the Russians get into space first. They were faulted for not integrating the nation ethnically" (p. 44). And now the schools are being blamed for the economic meltdown our nation has experienced. Contrary to what policymakers purport, educators are not responsible for the economic issues and woes of our nation today. The policymakers are, in fact, the ones who made those economic decisions.

Certainly the global economy has allowed them to make such decisions. However, policymakers have the responsibility to protect our nation's economy. Instead, their policy decisions have been about growing the wealth of a few, as well as their own power. Yet it is baffling how these same policymakers then blame educators for the economy they themselves created. For example, by blaming educators entirely, they have removed themselves from any role of responsibility in addressing poverty, but poverty has been identified by the research as a strong predictor of failure in children's learning. Although educators should never use this as an excuse for inaction, neither should policymakers. It is policymakers' responsibility to address the plight of children in poverty, who live in drug-infested, violent neighborhoods; parents unable or unwilling to take care of their children during nonschool hours; abuse in the homes; and inadequate food or health care—even as educators focus on helping all children to learn. Policymakers have allowed steadily increasing legal immigration (Nowak, n.d.) and rampant illegal immigration. Thus, schools have been overwhelmed by large numbers of children without language skills, but receive little or no support—only blame—when these children do not achieve on tests at the same level as native English speakers.

There are deep-seated issues with the changing ideology of our nation over which schools have no control and which policymakers choose to ignore. Bracey (2002) pointed out this ideology:

> The United States is the most economically stratified nation in the Western developed world. A 1994 study found that the top 1 percent of American families controlled 43 percent of the wealth, compared to 18 percent in Great Britain, the next most stratified country. That study also found that the salary ratio of the top 10 percent of workers in most countries was somewhere between 2:1 and 3:1. In the United States, it was 6:1. (p. 42)

What possible educational change can erase the effects of this economic ideology and the concomitant culture it nurtures? While policymakers pound their podiums demanding educational change that will improve job options in the future, they ignore the fact that the majority of jobs are becoming low-paying service jobs (Bracey 2002, 2006). Bracey (2002) pointed out the illogical connection demanded by policymakers of student performance in schools with a nation's economic state, citing, for example, the fact that Japanese students performed well on tests, while the Japanese economy declined.

In earlier work, I defined courageous leadership as comprised of wisdom, passion, and hope (Batagiannis, 2007). But today school leadership has been weakened, even as educators struggle to maintain it. The capacity exists for teachers, principals, and superintendents to lead the movement for substantive change in education, using their experience, research, and—most importantly—the dispositions of authenticity and care about children and learning. But that is not being allowed to happen. It is a challenge to remain hopeful in the face of state and national attacks on public education with *Race to the Top* and, for example, Fast Forward (Indiana's response). Sadly, the excitement of bright graduate students studying to be future leaders is being smothered and replaced by trepidation, fueled by the negative effects of policymakers' attacks on teachers and public schools. It is, indeed, heartbreaking to listen to their words about the loss of teaching creativity that has already been perpetrated on teachers and leaders and their honest consideration of leaving the field. It is disheartening to see aspiring leaders reduced to managers in the short span of time since the passage of NCLB. Hence, we run the risk that many of the most effective current and future leaders will be pushed out, leaving only the technical managers, who quip, "Just tell me what to do." The latter are the ones the policymakers are courting.

Myopic policymakers and those who do not demonstrate an authentic care for children or learning are ignoring their own inauthenticity; to use Obama's (2006) words, "And sometimes our ideological predispositions are just so fixed that we have trouble seeing the obvious" (p. 72). The widespread insistence that we follow the business model and subscribe to the claim that the market will solve all ills raises the question: How are those demands reconciled with the economic catastrophe we are experiencing, resulting from those very same business models?

As discussed earlier, policymakers have increasingly chosen to ignore the dispositions of teaching and leadership. They reject dispositions because they are not easily quantified or reduced to simplistic assessment and technical terms—and because they do not reflect the market mentality espoused by policymakers. However, Darling-Hammond (2009), flirting with hope once again, touched on the essence of dispositions and related the disposition of authenticity to Obama and his potential: "I believe Obama's administration has the opportunity to transform our nation's schools. The reasons have as much to do with the President himself as with his plans, as comprehensive and strategic as those might be" (p. 210). But the accuracy of her hopeful conclusion is dependent on the disposition of authenticity, the level of courage, and whether Obama has both. As discussed earlier, what he professes—if not reflected in his actions—is mere rhetoric. The rhetoric of the presidential campaign still echoes in the wings, but action is now necessary. Thus, while Obama has the intelligence to wordsmith and to speak eloquently, he must have the courage to act authentically on his own words. Continuing to raise doubts, however, are his actions and those of his staff, specifically those of Arne Duncan, which are discussed in a later section. Once again, these actions are in direct opposition to Obama's promises and his expressed dispositions, including authenticity, which Americans believed were reflected in his promises.

Educational Policy: Deep versus Technical Learning

Kanpol (1994) warned that teachers should focus on *educating*, not *schooling* their children. Particularly in the past decade, however, technical schooling is what is increasingly demanded of schools. Now teachers are evaluated not on whether they are "good" teachers, as any reasonable person might define the term, but rather on how obediently they follow the schooling curriculum. Giroux (2009) summarized the seeming narrowness of Obama's views on this subject:

> Obama's largely instrumental view of education appears to overlook the legacy of the nation's most prominent educational leaders and philosophers, including Thomas Jefferson, Horace Mann, John Dewey, W.E.B. Du Bois, Anna Julia Cooper, and Jane Addams, who valued education as a preeminent force for preparing young people to be socially responsible, critically engaged citizens in a democratic society. (p. 258)

This instrumental view reflected in policy is in contradiction to Obama's (2006) articulated claims, which actually acknowledged deep, complex issues and railed against the simplistic and the technical: "After all, the problems…are not simply technical problems in search of the perfect ten-point plan" (p. 254).

Accompanying the reduction of education to the simplistic and the technical, educators, too, are unappreciated; they are insulted and demeaned at every turn by policymakers. Reflecting this attitude and, at best, the technical, a governor dubbed pedagogy as "mumbo jumbo" as he pushed hard for his political agenda diminishing or eliminating the requirements of pedagogy and licensing for educators, reducing learning to teach to just passing a test, and eliminating the stable funding of public education ("Stormy Times Ahead," 2009). It is such hard-nosed politics that should lead one to ask: Have we lost the democracy of which we were so proud? Should a politician be able to dismiss entire bodies of knowledge and learning, for example, the pedagogy of teaching and learning, by virtue of the power of a political office? Giroux (2009), too, reminds the Obama administration that it "must understand…that the crisis in education is not only an economic problem…but also a political and ethical crisis about the very nature of citizenship and democracy" (p. 262).

As discussed earlier, Obama has dashed educators' hopes of changing NCLB and its deleterious effects on learning with his response of *Race to the Top* linked to money desperately needed by public schools to survive. Obama's current actions belie very different dispositions from those his rhetoric led us to expect. Perhaps, in part, this is a reflection of his desire to break the stronghold of partisanship. However, he can only be successful to a degree. He cannot eliminate the ideology behind certain partisan positions. Compromise is sometimes a good thing, but not when it requires that one sell one's soul. And there rests the dialectic of compromise/reducing partisanship and the absence of courage and authenticity in leadership. Obama (2006) seems to have forgotten once again his own words, "to distinguish between what can and cannot be compromised" (p. 51). Giroux (2009) pointed this out as well:

> The issue that Obama seems to miss in his concern with educational reform is that all educational ideals are not the same. Some ideals are well worth fighting for, and others should be rejected because they are at odds with any viable definition of schools as crucial democratic public spheres. (p. 256)

Giroux (2009) focused on the heart of the problem and the apparent absence of the disposition of authenticity reflected in Obama's actions:

> [There is] a serious disconnect between Obama's emphasis on education for public service and social responsibility and the neoliberal policies at the heart of the reform efforts he supports. This disconnect has distressing implications for how education policy will play out—or perhaps sell out—during his administration. ("Educating for What?" para 9)

Obama's (2006) book and his rhetoric indicated a disposition for change, for collaboration and a respect for the voices of all, and for closing the achievement gap. What, then, is at the root of these multiple contradictions and Obama's failure to act? Has his effort to appear bipartisan caused him to remain on the fence and to miss leadership opportunities? Dispositions and lack of authenticity are not the reasons, if one believes what he told us. However, at least the absence of courage seems to be. A prominent, retired university educator who campaigned hard for him recently described him as lacking courage.

Dionne (2010) encouraged Obama to discuss his beliefs to avoid confusing voters in his effort to be bipartisan and attempted to address the "contradictions of Obamaism," pointing out that he is "avoiding arguments over philosophy and ideology" (para 7), contrary to his own words:

> A second, more intimate theme to this book—namely, how I, or anybody in public office, can avoid the pitfalls of fame…and thereby retain that kernel of truth, that singular voice within each of us that reminds us of our deepest commitments….It is the language of values that people use to map their world. It is what can inspire them to take action, and move them beyond their isolation. (Obama, 2006, pp. 15, 64)

But authenticity both of beliefs and actions is necessary and sadly seems lacking in President Obama. His own words again confirmed the importance of authenticity: "After all, talk is cheap, like any value, empathy must be acted upon" (Obama, 2006, p. 83). How then does he ignore the effects of policies that lead, for example, to the even more onerous scripting of teaching and leading, which, in turn, contributes to the deskilling of teachers and school leaders (Kanpol, 1994, 2002) to the detriment of children, especially children in poverty, who are most adversely affected?

Educational Policy: Private or Public Good

Education is not a private good, but a public one (Bracey, 2002; Giroux, 2009; Ravitch, 2010). The dispositions reflecting the desire to move away from any interest in community and the public good are motivated by individual, selfish interests. Bracey (2002) criticized the privatization of education and the focus on jobs that supports privatization: "Given all this emphasis on jobs, it is not surprising that many people have stopped viewing education as a public good…and have started viewing it simply as another market to be exploited" (p. 15).

Obama (2006) himself strongly denounced privatization:

> But over the long term, doing nothing probably means an America very different from the one most of us grew up in. It will mean a nation even more stratified economically and socially than it currently is: one in which an increasingly prosperous knowledge class, living in exclusive enclaves, will be able to purchase whatever they want on the marketplace—private schools, private health care, private security, and private jets—while a growing number of their fellow citizens are consigned to low-paying service jobs, vulnerable to dislocation, pressed to work longer hours, dependent on an underfunded, overburdened, and underperforming public sector for their health care, their retirement, and their children's educations. (pp. 175–176)

Policymakers have supported charter schools in what appears to be an interim step before total privatization of education. Although they cannot fund one set of public schools, they have created a second one, which they also choose to call *public schools*. When pressed for evaluation of their programs, the charter school managers often decry their problems, which sound no different than the challenges experienced by public schools (Bracey, 2002). Merrow (2009) reported Ravitch's comments on the direction of Washington "reform," including charters, specifically:

> To me, the problem here is obvious: What if Washington doesn't know best? What if the "reform" ideas are wrong? As I said before, the CREDO study at Stanford—which looked at performance in half the nation's charters—found that 80% or more of charter schools are no better than or worse than their neighborhood public school. Why replace struggling public schools with worse charter schools? There is a ton of evidence that evaluating teachers based solely on student test scores is a bad idea. ("He's Using the Money," para 2)

Clearly, policymakers have been wrong in the blame they have heaped on schools in order to avoid their own responsibility. Authenticity would require them to admit that schools and educators are not the ones who are responsible for the multitude of social problems for which schools are blamed: poverty, violence, drugs, and so on. Educators are, in fact, the ones who have always taken on every social problem because it affects "our kids." Good teachers and leaders have gone into education in the past not because it was a job, but rather a mission, a way to improve the lives of children and society. Instead of garnering appreciation for their dedication and hard work, they are criticized and demeaned for not fixing all the ills that are not about education, but social ills for which policymakers refuse to take responsibility. Policymakers should be reminded of the subjects that have become the responsibility of schools over the years, in addition to learning: drug education, because policymakers could not eradicate drugs from the community; feeding children, because policymakers could not resolve the growing issues of poverty; violence, not because it began in the schools, but because policymakers could not address violence and the poverty that fed it in the community; sex education, because parents were not addressing it in the home; and health issues, medical services, and counseling services, because children needed them, and there were no community provisions. And the list goes on.

And of the market, Obama (2006) said: "There is the absolutism of the free market, an ideology of no taxes, no regulations, no safety net" (p. 46). Giroux (2009) points to the contradictions: "The puzzling disparity between Obama's call for curbing the excesses of free-market fundamentalism in the realm of economics, while at the same time supporting the use of market-driven protocols to structure his educational policies, needs to be brought to light and challenged if a more democratic political culture has hope of taking root in the United States" ("Educating for What?" para 9). So one cannot help but ask: Where is this Obama now who is permitting Duncan to march the nation in the direction of privatizing education—and the very America of which Obama's words warned us?

Educational Policy: Individualism and Politics or Community

Privatization is strongly linked to overly exuberant individualism and the neglect of our national community. Being authentic about education requires understanding the purpose of education, including its relationship to democracy and community; acting on those beliefs; and resisting the conflicting and often inauthentic battles of individualism over education. Long before the era in which we now live, Goodlad, in *What Schools Are For* (1979), concluded that, as a result of individualism, "the democratic community is at risk....We sacrificed social capital to financial capital, making the latter more and more the goal of heightened individualism" (p. x). He then criticized policymakers—even at that point in our history—for focusing on individualism and no longer democracy and, thus, thwarting the role of schools:

> And the rhetoric of federal and state educational policy and reform massage and assuage this rampant individualism, making it even more difficult for local schools to serve the democratic purposes for which they were and, presumably, still are intended. (p. x)

Obama (2006), in speaking of values, also addressed the disposition of commitment to community: "All of which raises the question: What are the core values that we, as Americans, hold in common?" (p. 63). He identified "our communal values, our sense of mutual responsibility and social solidarity" (p. 77). Finally, he acknowledged that there is a dialectic between individualism and community: "In every society (and in every individual), these twin strands—the individualistic and the communal, autonomy and solidarity—are in tension" (p. 67). Obama continued, identifying the necessary balancing of the two:

> Our individualism has always been bound by a set of communal values, the glue upon which every healthy society depends....And we value the constellation of behaviors that express our mutual regard for one another: honesty, fairness, humility, kindness, courtesy, and compassion. (p. 67)

And he even quickly pointed out the pitfalls of forgetting the fact that we are a society and a community and allowing individualism to prevail:

> At times our values collide because in the hands of men each one is subject to distortion and excess. Self-reliance and independence can transform into selfishness and license, ambition into greed and a frantic desire to succeed at any cost. (p. 69)

Obama also pointed out the loss of community that can result from power, an extension of individualism, particularly in the political scene: "I was reminded of the dangerous isolation that power can bring, and appreciated the Founders' wisdom in designing a system to keep power in check" (p. 56). He pointed out the selfish interest embedded in the seeking of power: "I'm reminded that the actions of those in power have enormous consequences—a price that they themselves almost never have to pay" (p. 59). Obama criticized Congress: "In the world's greatest deliberative body, no one is listening" (p. 19). Yet he himself is not listening to educators.

Policymakers have dismissed educators and their concerns, claiming we are afraid of change. That is not so. I cite my own experience as one example of the inauthenticity of policymakers in addressing change in education. The prevailing agenda in the 1990s for every political candidate was to become the educational congressperson, governor, or president. "School improvement" became the new buzzword. Yet when, as a new superintendent passionate about school improvement, I asked a candidate for State Superintendent of Public Instruction in 1992 what resources would be available, I was told, "None." When I called the Indiana Department of Education in 1991 with a plan for English-as-a-second-language students, the person responsible for the program applauded my ideas. When I naively asked about resources as a new superintendent in a district already strapped for money, I was told there were none. Yet now educators are attacked by policymakers, who scurry to claim credit, as if educators have had no vision and made no such attempts to effect change. Since policymakers are enthralled with international comparisons, they should examine the respect with which educators and education are treated in Finland and Japan, for instance.

Of politics generally, Obama (2006) concluded: "Politics today is a business and not a mission" (p. 31). And yet he is allowing education to be reduced to a business, as well, and educators to be degraded and ultimately chased away—educators who indeed entered the field as a mission—to use Obama's own words. Thus, as discussed throughout this chapter, Obama (2006) has expressed the dispositions that resulted in his election, including deep authenticity, and acknowledged the value of dispositions:

> At the core of the American experience are a set of ideals that continue to stir our collective conscience; a common set of values that bind us together despite our differences; a running thread of hope that makes our improbable experiment in democracy work. (2006, p. 11)

But his actions remain contradictory and, therefore, seem to be inauthentic.

Ultimate Contradiction in Policy: Obama's Choice of Secretary of Education—Arne Duncan

When Obama considered Linda Darling-Hammond for the position of Secretary of Education, hope surged among educators. She is an educator and a respected educational reformer. The tide indeed seemed to have turned; the voice of educators was actually to be included. As Obama considered whom to select as Secretary of Education, some warned him not to pick one who would support the "status quo," "weaker" reform, or "superficial" reform (Kohn, 2008). But those so warning Obama quite simply did not want an educator appointed. The self-proclaimed "reformers" were those who supported the privatization of education. Is it any wonder that both Rod Paige and Margaret Spellings applauded Duncan's selection as Secretary of Education? Margaret Spellings pronounced herself "thrilled" with the selection, while Rod Paige called Duncan "a budding hero in the education business" (Kohn, 2008). Chester Finn, longtime critic of public education, also applauded Duncan. After all, they, too, share some of what I term deficient dispositions when it comes to education, which were characteristic of the last two Secretaries of Education and are now exhibited by Duncan as well.

Thus, hope began to evaporate with the appointment of Arne Duncan. Doubts were grounded in his dispositions and his history, and the introduction of *Race to the Top* confirmed these doubts. In analyzing the authenticity of leaders, honesty in their leadership actions is expected. Former Secretary of Education Rod Paige claimed that, as the superintendent of the Houston schools, he had led his district to improved achievement, yet that did not prove to be the case when the claims were questioned. The Texas Education Agency audited Houston records and concluded:

> Some 3,000 of 5,500 students who left school in the 2000–2001 school year, or 54 percent, should have been reported as dropouts, but were not. That year, the 212,000-student Houston system reported a dropout rate of 1.5 percent…that contributed, along with climbing test scores, to the city's reputation as a showcase for the "Texas miracle" in education. (Schemo, 2003, paras 6–7)

Now Duncan is in that same national leadership position. Diane Ravitch (2009b) asked:

> If Arne Duncan knows exactly how to reform American education, why didn't he reform Chicago's schools? A report came out a couple of weeks ago from the Civic

> Committee of Chicago ("Still Left Behind") saying that Chicago's much-touted score gains in the past several years were phony, that they were generated after the state lowered the passing mark on the state tests, that the purported gains did not show up on the federal tests, and that Chicago's high schools are still failing....Chicago continues to be one of the lowest performing cities in the nation on the NAEP. ("Tell Me More," para 1)

So we have been led in the past and are currently being led by individuals who did not achieve what they have demanded of schools. It also seems that under their leadership not only was the purported achievement absent, but so was honesty. Furthermore, how can policymakers demand what they found impossible? The answer, it seems, lies in the problematic emphasis of current public policy on "the three horsemen of the new apocalypse—management, money, and marketing" (Eyre, 2003, as cited in Nixon, 2004)—and the resulting inauthenticity among policymakers.

As for Arne Duncan, what does he bring to the table that makes him omniscient? Power does not equal wisdom after all. On what basis does he dismiss all educators as incompetent? Trite as this challenge may sound, it truly might help if Duncan and other noneducators who wish to lead would enter the classroom as teachers, not critics from afar. That would provide an opportunity for them to model their demands and to be evaluated on that basis.

Duncan is not an educator; he has never taught. What are his educational qualifications? A mayor appointed him, and then a president. That makes him a politician. He had no preparation or experience as an educator when he was appointed to "lead" the Chicago Public Schools. Our current times reflect one of the worst eras for the inauthentic use and abuse of language in an effort to harness the power of words. Thus, although he has only political appointments, Duncan is suddenly also touted by some of his supporters as an educational reformer. One must examine the reasons for that definition, who so defines him, and their own dispositions.

Arne Duncan does not support public education, as evidenced consistently by his words and actions. He is, in fact, an avid supporter of privatization, and his definition of reform is narrow, superficial, and reflective of his personal agenda. As one example of his philosophical stance, Giroux (2009) points to Duncan's organization of a symposium, "Free to Choose, Free to Succeed: The New Market in Public Education." The guests consisted of business representatives, proponents of privatization, and members of conservative think tanks; there were no educators invited. Duncan talks about the arts but then does not support schools in anything but the technocrat's language of "laser-like focus on academics" ("Free to Choose," para 6), which leaves no time for the arts. He speaks of closing the achievement gap and yet fails to reconcile the contradictions when urban schools have been reduced to scripted teaching. Years ago when I was teaching English as a new teacher in a school, I reviewed the curriculum for non-college-bound students and was horrified that we were allowing students to graduate with more of the "basics" deemed important, but without reading one work of drama. We quickly corrected that error, but today a narrow curriculum, defined by such as Duncan, is not only becoming universal, but is designated not as an error but as "reform." Yet Obama (2006) criticized the straying from the disposition of authenticity by misusing language: "We know how high-flying words can be deployed in the service of cynical aims, and how the noblest sentiments can be subverted in the name of power, expedience, greed, or intolerance" (p. 12).

Duncan exemplifies these words. He verbalizes what seems to indicate appropriate leadership dispositions and appears politically correct, as, for example, in talking about teachers and altruism, but he quickly reverts to comments about how "bad" schools are—painting all schools with a broad brush. In analyzing a video presentation of Duncan (2009) in which he addressed the topic of recruiting teachers, my graduate students pointed out that he identified multiple potential sources for teacher candidates, but made no mention of one—current teachers—indicating once again his lack of respect for them.

Having the power to close and reopen schools and to implement a militaristic model, as Duncan did in Chicago, does not make him a reformer. Yet it is no surprise that Duncan cannot focus on authentic, deep reform. After all, he lacks the experience, study of education, and resulting understanding of children, learning, and education to do more than tinker with reform. Because he has the power to make changes, but lacks the necessary understanding, any change has equal merit in his eyes as he adopts one quick fix after the other. Duncan lacks the *wisdom* of courageous leadership. Instead, he is proud of the fact that he is doing "stuff," but there is nothing remarkable in implementing superficial ideas, some in direct contradiction to the very research he claims to espouse. In fact, it is dangerous to education and to our American society.

In contrast, Darling-Hammond (2009) commented on Obama's presumed disposition of authenticity and vision: "I was pleasantly surprised by his appetite for comprehensiveness rather than a quick-fix approach bound to be partial and inadequate" (para 4). Yet Duncan personifies the contradiction to those very words in his "race" for instantaneous perfection. Giroux and Saltman (2008) criticized Duncan, as well as Obama for appointing him,

> not only because Duncan largely defines schools within a market-based and penal model of pedagogy, but also because he does not have the slightest understanding of schools as something other than adjuncts of the corporation at best or the prison at worse [*sic*]. (para 2)

Ravitch (2009b), too, pointedly criticized Obama for appointing Duncan:

> However, based on what I have seen to date, I conclude that Obama has given President George W. Bush a third term in education policy and that Arne Duncan is the male version of Margaret Spellings....We all know that Secretary Spellings greeted Duncan's appointment with glee. (para 3)

Thus, Duncan's dispositions show beneath the "hem" of his political attire. One must wonder if President Obama, too, will continue—contrary to his own dispositions—to support the last best, superficial magic bullet disguised as reform, the more-of-the-same, thoughtless action. President Obama now must determine if hope or cynicism will be the hallmark of his leadership in education discussed in the concluding section.

Conclusion: Which Road Will President Obama Choose: Descent into Cynicism or Reigniting of Hope?

In conclusion, we now stand as a nation and a citizenry at the fork in the road, reminiscent of Robert Frost's (1915) poem "The Road Not Taken." We can take "the one less traveled," the road of authenticity, which reflects honesty, the truthfulness of the children in *The Emperor's New Clothes*, who didn't hesitate to say the emperor was not wearing any clothes. This road will reignite hope in our nation. The other choice is the easier, more frequently traveled road of inauthenticity; it represents a descent into cynicism and is symbolized by the nonexistent clothes that all were expected to "see" in the fairy tale. It is the one currently travelled by so many policymakers, but "paid" for by citizens.

The road of inauthenticity will lead us to more of the same: increasing privatization; growing commitment to individualism; worshiping of the market, continuing to allow obscene amounts of wealth to be amassed by a few at the expense of the broader American society; identifying and discarding those unable to maneuver and survive the market; emphasizing technical schooling over education and increasingly controlled by policymakers; deskilling teachers and educational leaders, and increasing punitive measures in order to control citizens. At the end of this road of inauthenticity, our democracy is at serious risk of failing.

If President Obama leads us down the road of authenticity, that road will be one of a democratic community in which we value and respect each other as human beings. There will be an end to the overt and covert war against public education. A genuine, thoughtful plan of reform will be developed, as opposed to the promotion of competition, with its mentality of losers and winners. Education will be valued and supported as a public good, offering opportunity to every child. An educator will be appointed to the position of Secretary of Education, who understands the deep issues, complexities, and dispositions of teaching and educational leadership and with the capacity to implement authentic reform rather than to tinker with surface issues. Instead of making superficial comparisons, policymakers will learn from countries such as Finland and note that Finland recruits and retains the strongest educators, educates them well, respects them, and gives them the freedom to teach. Education, not schooling, will be the emphasis, something for which the United States was emulated by other countries in the days before NCLB and *Race to the Top*. Educators will be respected for their work, not blamed for social ills beyond their control. Indicative of this respect, educators and policymakers will join hands to meet today's new challenges, focusing on the overarching goal of teaching children to love learning, to problem solve, to think deeply and critically, and to be good citizens. At the end of that road, although it will not be an easy one, our democracy, founded on public education, will remain strong.

This chapter indeed has contrasted President Obama's professed authenticity with the contradictions in his actions and policies. He summarized these challenges himself (Obama, 2006) as he reflected on authenticity and politics, the pressure of inauthenticity, and the reality of those in politics who have ultimately succumbed to inauthenticity. Although he cannot lead without courage and authenticity, it is time for President Obama to remember that he did not say "I," but "We," when he spoke of change. He should reflect on his original invitation to the nation when he challenged us to work with him to effect change. Indeed, we do not expect him to do this alone. We accepted the invitation and stand ready to work with him. Together, *Yes, We Can* travel the road of authenticity.

I remain hopeful that the American Dream my parents pursued and deeply valued will remain part of our nation's present and future, as well as its history. I supported the election of President Obama, and I believe that his leadership founded on his authenticity and courage can indeed reignite hope in our nation and recommit the nation to the American Dream founded on public education.

Notes

Chapter Four

1 Chapter 4 was previously published; some revisions have been made to the original publication. Permission has been granted for republication: Batagiannis, S. C. (2010). Obama's educational policy: Disposition of authenticity or the politics of *The Emperor's New Clothes*. *Journal of Educational Thought*, *44*(3), 229–257.

2 *Instantaneous perfection* is a term I ignited in education to reflect the demands of our society for quick and perfect solutions that translate into simplistic searches for magic bullets.

3 NCATE: National Council for Accreditation in Teacher Education.

4 INTASC: Interstate New Teacher Assessment and Support Consortium.

5 ISLLC: Interstate School Leaders Licensure Consortium developed the ISLLC Standards for educational leaders in 1996.

References

Batagiannis, S.C. (2007). Leadership guided by courage: A challenge to instantaneous perfection. *Journal of Educational Thought*, *41*(2), 145–164.

Berliner, D.C., & Biddle, B.J. (1995). *The manufactured crisis: Myths, fraud, and the attack on America's public schools.* New York: Addison-Wesley.

Bogen, M. (2007, July/August). In search of that "third thing." *Harvard Education Letter*, *23*(4), 4–6.

Bracey, G.W. (2002). *The war against America's public schools*. Boston: Allyn & Bacon.

———. (2006, December). Students do NOT need high-level skills in today's job market. *Education Digest*, *72*(4), 24–28.

Compact Oxford English dictionary of current English. Retrieved June 23, 2010, from http://www.askoxford.com/concise_oed/authentic?view=uk

Council of Chief State School Officers. (1992). Interstate New Teachers Assessment and Support Consortium of the Council of Chief State School Officers. *Model standards for beginning teacher licensing, assessment and development: A resource for state dialogue.* Retrieved April 27, 2010, from http://www.ccsso.org/content/pdfs/corestrd.pdf

———. (1996). *Interstate School Leaders Licensure Consortium standards for school leaders*. Retrieved March 21, 2010, from http://www.ccsso.org/content/pdfs/isllcstd.pdf

———. (2008). ISLLC Standards 2008 FAQs. Retrieved March 21, 2010, from http://www.ccso.org/projects/education_leadership_initiatives/ISLLC_Standards_2008_FAQs/#comparison2

Darling-Hammond, L. (2009). President Obama and education: The possibility for dramatic improvement in teaching and learning. *Harvard Educational Review*, *79*(2), 210–223.

Dionne, E.J., Jr. (2010). The contradictions of Obamaism. *truthout*. Retrieved January 21, 2010, from http://www.truthout.org/ej-dionne-jr-the-contradictions-obamaism56238

Duncan, A. (2009, March 26). Education Secretary Arne Duncan on teacher prep programs and teachers' unions. *Education Week*. Retrieved May 12, 2010, from http://www.youtube.com/watch?v=QrzuQn6KB0A

Foster, W. (1986). *Paradigms and promises*. Amherst, NY: Prometheus Books.

Frost, Robert. (1915). The road not taken. Retrieved June 22, 2010, from http://www.amandashome.com/road.html

Fullan, M. (2005). *Leadership and sustainability*. Thousand Oaks, CA: Corwin.

Giroux, H.A. (2009, Summer). Obama's dilemma: Postpartisan politics and the crisis of American education. *Harvard Educational Review*, *79*(2), 250–266.

Giroux, H.A., & Saltman, K. (2008, December 17). Obama's betrayal of public education? Arne Duncan and the corporate model of schooling. *truthout*. Retrieved March 1, 2010, from http://www.truthout.org/121708R?print

Goldberg, M. (2005). Test mess 2: Are we doing better a year later? *Phi Delta Kappan*, *86*(5), 389–395.

Goodlad, J.I. (1979). *What schools are for*. Bloomington, IN: Phi Delta Kappa Educational Foundation.

———. (2007). Why we need public education. In C. Glickman (Ed.), *Letters to the next president* (pp. 54–60). New York: Teachers College Press.

Hargreaves, A., & Fink, D. (2006). *Sustainable leadership*. San Francisco: Jossey-Bass.

Heifetz, R. (1994). *A leadership without easy answers*. Cambridge, MA: Belknap Press of Harvard University.

High school graduation rates in Washington and the United States: A long-run view. (2005). *Washington State Institute for Public Policy*. Retrieved June 20, 2010, from http://www.wsipp.wa.gov/rptfiles/05-03-2201.pdf

Kanpol, B. (1994). *Critical pedagogy for beginning teachers: The movement from despair to hope*. Retrieved June 6, 2010, from http://www.lib.umwestern.edu/pub/jcp/issueII-1/kanpol.html

———. (2002, January). Critical educational leadership: Put up or shut up! *Educational Foundations*, *16*(1), 5–18.

Kanpol, B., & Yeo, F. (Eds.). (2000). *The academy and the possibility of belief.* Cresskill, NJ: Hampton Press.

King, W. (1996). *Hans Christian Andersen's fairy tales*. Philadelphia: Courage.

Kohn, A. (2008, December 29). Beware of school "reformers." *The Nation*. Retrieved June 16, 2010, from http://www.alfiekohn.org/teaching/soe.htm

Kozol, J. (2005a, November). American apartheid. *NEA Today*, *24*(3), 32–34.

———. (2005b). *The shame of the nation: The restoration of apartheid schooling in America.* New York: Crown.

Merrow, J. (2009, August). Privatization will not help us achieve our goals: An interview with Diane Ravitch. *Taking note: Thoughts on education from John Merrow*. Retrieved August 4, 2009, from http://learningmatters.tv/blog/op-ed/privatization-will-not-help-us-achieve-our-goals-an-interview-with-diane-ravitch/2413/

National Council for Accreditation of Teacher Education. (2006a, June 16). A statement from NCATE on professional dispositions. Retrieved May 16, 2010, from http://www.ncate.org/public/0616_MessageAWise.asp?ch=150

———. (2006b). Professional Standards 2006. Retrieved May 16, 2010, from http://www.ncate.org/documents/standards/ unit_stnds_2006.pdf

———. (2007, November 13). NCATE issues call for action; Defines professional dispositions as used in teacher education. *NCATE News*. Retrieved May 16, 2010, from http://www.ncate.org/public/102407.asp?ch=148

Nixon, J. (2004). Education for the good society: The integrity of academic practice. *London Review of Education*, *2*(3), 245–252.

Noddings, N. (1984). *Caring: A feminine approach to ethical moral education*. Berkeley: University of California Press.

Nowak, M.W. (n.d.). Immigration and U.S. population growth: An environmental perspective. *NPG Special Report.* Retrieved June 20, 2010, at http://www.npg.org/specialreports/imm&uspopgrowth.htm

Obama, B. (2006). *The audacity of hope: Thoughts on reclaiming the American dream.* New York: Vintage.

Ohanian, S. (1999). *One size fits few.* Portsmouth, NH: Heinemann.

Perkins, D. (1995). *Outsmarting IQ: The emerging science of learnable intelligence.* New York: The Free Press.

Petrilli, M. (July 2009). The Race to the Top: The carrot that feels like a stick. *Education Gadfly Flypaper.* Retrieved November 30, 2011, from http://www.educationgadfly.net/flypaper/2009/07/the-race-to-the-top-the-carrot-that-feels-like-a-stick/

Ravitch, D. (2009a, February 24). Is Arne Duncan really Margaret Spellings in drag? *Education Week. Bridging Differences,* para 3. Retrieved June 16, 2010, from http://blogs.edweek.org/edweek/BridgingDifferences/2009/02/is_arne_duncan_really_margaret.html

———. (2009b, August 4). Privatization will not help us achieve our goals: An interview with Diane Ravitch. *Taking Note: Thoughts on education from John Merrow.* Retrieved August 4, 2009, from http://learningmatters.tv/blog/op-ed/privatization-will-not-help-us-achieve-our-goals-an-interview-with-diane-ravitch/2413/

———. (2010). *The death and life of the great American school system.* New York: Basic Books, Perseus.

Ringe, D.L. (1950). Hawthorne's psychology of the head and the heart. *PMLA*, *65*, 120–132.

Ritchhart, R., & Perkins, D. (2008). Making things visible. *Educational Leadership*, *65*(5), 57–61.

Sagor, R. (2005). *The action research guidebook.* Thousand Oaks, CA: Corwin.

Schemo, D.J. (2003, August 8). State to monitor Houston schools to ensure reporting of dropouts. *The New York Times.* Retrieved June 6, 2010, from http://www.nytimes.com/2003/08/08/us/state-to-monitor-houston-schools-to-ensure-reporting-of-dropouts.html?fta=y?pagewanted=1

Sockett, H. (2009). Dispositions as virtues: The complexity of the construct. *Journal of Teacher Education*, *60*(3), 291–303.

Stormy times ahead for mumbo jumbo education talkers. (2009, July 26). *Education Policy Blog.* Retrieved June 2, 2010, from http://educationpolicyblog.blogspot.com/2009/07/stormy-times-ahead-for-mumbo-jumbo.html

Turkmen, H. (2009). Examining elementary science education teachers disposition after reform. *Asia-Pacific Forum on Science Learning and Teaching*, *10*(2). Available at http://www.ied.edu.hk/apfslt/v10_issue2/turkmen/turkmen2.htm

Usher, L., Usher, M., & Usher, D. (2003, November 20–21). *Nurturing five dispositions of effective teachers.* 2nd National Symposium on Educator Dispositions, Eastern Kentucky University, Richmond, KY. Retrieved May 16, 2010, from http://www.emich.edu/dartep/handouts/Dispositionsproceedingssession_P.pdf

Vannini, P. (2006). Dead poets' society: Teaching, publish-or-perish, and professors' experience of authenticity. *Symbolic Interaction*, *29*(2), 235–257.

Winchester, I. (2007). Editorial: The complexity of the educational enterprise. *Journal of Educational Thought*, *41*(2), 101–104.

Zhao, Y. (2009). *Catching up or leading the way*. Alexandria, VA: Association for Supervision and Curriculum Development.

❖ C H A P T E R   F I V E ❖

Obama Drama: A Play among Hope, Education, and Discontinuity

Marisol Rexach & Tom Wilson

On January 20, 2009, the United States witnessed the inauguration of Barack Hussein Obama as president. In a country where only 60 years ago education was divided along color lines with a "separate but equal" doctrine, the election of an African American president prompted many to recall a turning point in education: Brown versus the Board of Education of Topeka (*Brown v. Board of Education*, 347 U.S. 483, 1954).

The pre-Obama climate was rife with events that distracted our developing collective consciousness. Political events and changes in educational policy instigated a resurgence of the separate-but-equal mentality, which led to No Child Left Behind (NCLB). The NCLB Act of 2001 was signed into law on January 8, 2002, just 4 months after 9/11. Based on the theory that setting measurable objectives and high standards would improve educational outcomes, the act required each state to develop basic skills tests to be administered in schools with school funding related to assessments. Because NCLB did not assert national achievement standards, each state created its own standards. Not surprisingly, different levels of difficulty were subsequently found in cross-state comparison scores, leading to increased discussion as to the viability of nationally set standards (National Center for Education Statistics, 2007). Standardized tests were in full bloom. These norm-referenced tests delineated the haves and have-nots. The resultant term *achievement gap* served to demonstrate that poor students, Latino students, and African American students were consistently not proficient.

Clearly, these were challenging times. Faced with these political and educational challenges, Barack Obama promised a new vision for the United States. His message was simple: "Hope" and "Yes we can!" These straightforward phrases captured the essence of speeches that became the hallmark of his campaign. On July 27, 2004, Obama delivered a stirring speech at the Democratic National Convention. Then a senatorial candidate, his eloquence was recognized. Many contend that this speech was a defining moment in his political career. His message, it can be said, invoked a feeling of hope for many:

> For alongside our famous individualism, there's another ingredient in the American saga. A belief that we are connected as one people. If there's a child on the south side of Chicago who can't read, that matters to me, even if it's not my child. If there's a senior citizen somewhere who can't pay for her prescription and has to choose between medicine and the rent, that makes my life poorer, even if it's not my grandmother. If there's an Arab-American family being rounded up without benefit of an attorney or due process, that threatens my civil liberties. It's that fundamental belief—I am my brother's keeper, I am my sister's keeper that makes this country work. It's what allows us to pursue our individual dreams, yet still come together as a single American family. "E pluribus unum." Out of many, one. (Obama, 2004)

The articulateness of Barack Obama, when placed in juxtaposition to the events of the Bush legacy, clearly conveyed a message of authenticity, possibility, and audacity in his suggestion of a willingness to take bold risks. In *The Audacity of Hope*, Obama (2006) explains: "That was the best of the American spirit…having the audacity to believe despite all the evidence to the contrary….It was that audacity, I thought, that joined us as one people" (p. 356). Obama also affirms:

> I am a Democrat, after all; my views on most topics correspond more closely to the editorial pages of the *New York Times* than those of the *Wall Street Journal*. I am angry about policies that consistently favor the wealthy and powerful over average Americans, and insist that government has an important role in opening up opportunity to all. I believe in evolution, scientific inquiry, and global warming; I believe in free speech, whether politically correct or politically incorrect, and I am suspicious of using government to impose anybody's religious beliefs—including my own—or nonbelievers. (p. 10)

From these declarations, those of us who sensed the dangers of a regressive post-9/11, NCLB ideology felt the passionate pull of his prose and his democratic and progressive stance. We celebrated the appointment of Stanford University's Linda Darling-Hammond to lead his educational advisory transition team. This appointment seemed to be in tune with the promises of *The Audacity of Hope*. However, when Darling-Hammond was not appointed Secretary of Education, we experienced a further cognitive itch. In an attempt to alleviate the discomfort, it became necessary to take a closer look at the educational writing in *The Audacity of Hope*. Although the election of Obama marked a possible change in the collective ideology of the country, the appointment of Arne Duncan as Secretary of Education and the implementation of Race to the Top have stalled that possibility.

This re-reading reinforced our misgivings about his educational rhetoric. Increasingly, particularly at the level of language, there appeared to be a disconnect between his beliefs about social, forward-looking democratic change, and his support for what many perceived to be a regressive educational discourse characterized as unmitigated faith in technology, high-stakes testing, national and state standards, and—probably most significant—competitive economic efficacy.

So how might this perceived continuation of the Bush approach to educational reform be explained? To answer this question, we begin with a brief explication of keyword discourse research followed by a description of Milton Rokeach's (1973) foundational study centered on the values of freedom and equality (operationalized as keywords) from the texts of authors representing four political ideologies: democratic socialism, fascism, conservatism/capitalism, and communism. Our keyword research begins with an analysis of these four political ideologies in order to establish reference points for analyzing Obama's political ideology. Once in office, he was accused of having socialist—if not communist and even fascist—tendencies. Through an analysis of his speeches, we see that, although Obama's message of community does pervade his discourse, his political ideology, at least by our criteria, is centrist and mainstream. As we will see later, a communist or a fascist he is not.

Then we expand the meaning of democratic discourse by including, with justification, two additional keywords of community and democracy in order to assess the frequency and percentage of these four keywords within two major educational texts (Wilford Aiken's *The Story of the Eight Year Study* and Ted Sizer's *Horace's Compromise*) and three literary texts (Martin Luther King Jr.'s "Letter from a Birmingham Jail" and "I Have a Dream," and Jonathon Kozol's *Savage Inequalities*).

We apply the lessons learned from these nine samples to examine President Obama's educational ideology as revealed by the frequency of use of the four keywords (freedom, equality, community, and democracy) within 71 speeches, of which 11 were devoted specifically to education. Simply stated, our interest is to determine the degree to which his educational language compares to our nine previous samples. Finally, we move beyond keyword analysis to gain an understanding of his belief about the ultimate aim of education based on a close reading of *The Audacity of Hope*.

Keyword Discourse and Political Ideologies

Wilson (2000[1]) cites Michel Foucault (as cited in Ball, 1990), who writes of discourses that are about what can be said and thought, but also who can speak, when, and with what authority. Meanings are derived, then, not so much from languages but from contexts with their historical, institutional practices and power relationships. In addition, discourses constrain the possibilities of thought beyond what can be said; they are about what cannot be said. Thus, they are constituted by exclusion as well as inclusion.

Raymond Williams (1983) calls our attention to the importance of keywords "we share with others, often imperfectly, when we wish to discuss many of the central processes of our common life" (p. 14). Keywords are necessary for an understanding of our society and reflect the values within that society. At any given time, certain words cluster to constitute a particular discourse as "elements of an active vocabulary—a way of recording, investigating and presenting problems of meaning in the area of in which the meanings…have formed" (p. 15).

In discussing meaning as above, Foucault (as cited in Ball, 1990) seems to privilege context over language itself, yet Williams (1983) is not so sure. There is more to it than time and place, wherein:

> The problem of meaning can never be wholly dissolved into context. It is true that no word ever stands on its own, since it is always an element in the social process of language, and its uses depend upon the complex and (though variably) systematic properties of language itself. Yet it can still be useful to pick out certain words, of an especially problematic kind and to consider, for the moment, their own internal development and structures. (Williams, 1983, pp. 22–23)

For our keyword task here, the political value conceptualization and methodology of Milton Rokeach (1973) are central. He defines a value as "an enduring belief that an end-state of existence is personally or socially preferable to an opposite or converse mode end-state of existence" (p. 5). He assumes that individuals differ not so much on the possession of values *per se,* which are relatively small in number, but rather on the importance they lend to particular values in relationship to other values. The rank order or hierarchy of terminal values on a "continuum of perceived importance," then, constitutes a value system.

Examples of terminal values follow. The words in parenthesis are "value categories" that expand the meaning of the particular value:

- A comfortable life (a prosperous life),
- Freedom (independence, free choice),
- Equality (brotherhood, equal opportunity for all), and
- True friendship (close companionship).

The question then becomes one of ascertaining how Rokeach's efforts could inform our examination of democratic discourse in school reform movements. He argues that political ideology, in terms of a liberal-conservative dichotomy, is not a phenomenon that can be ordered along a single continuum but rather is best understood as a "language of values" (p. 168), incorporating the two values *freedom* and *equality* from the list of terminal values. He writes:

> It may be hypothesized that all major varieties of political orientation will have to take an explicitly favorable, a silent, or an explicitly unfavorable position with respect to two values in particular—*freedom and equality*—...[and] the major variations in political ideology are hypothesized to be fundamentally reducible, when stripped to the barest essence, to opposing value orientations concerning the political desirability of *freedom and equality* in all their ramifications. (p. 169; italics original)

As previously noted, the meaning of keywords needs to be understood in their relationship within a given context (Foucault, as cited in Ball, 1990) and at the same time honored for their internal development and structure (Williams, 1983). What, then, are the meanings of freedom and equality in analysis? The definitions that Rokeach (1973) offers for equality (with its attending "categories" of brotherhood, equal opportunity for all) and freedom (with its "categories" of independence and free choice) further indicate his sense of the two keywords. Yet he sees them in terms of each other, wherein "the meaning of freedom and equality is to be sought in their relation to one another within a particular set of values" (Rokeach, 1973, p. 183). It is the contextual inclusion and strong emphasis of *both* equality and freedom that characterize a democratic vocabulary and discourse.

When the texts of Goldwater, Hitler, and Lenin were examined, a keywords' frequency analysis revealed that, for the socialists, both freedom (66) and equality (62) are essentially the same. Goldwater (capitalism) used freedom 85 times, yet equality at minus 10. This pattern is reversed for Lenin (communism), with equality at 88 and freedom at negative 47. The results demonstrate the value of keyword research. Despite the varying ideologies examined, we see a clear correlation with the frequency of keyword usage and the ideological stance of the individual. Quite clearly, a profile of one's philosophy surfaces; it cannot hide. For Hitler (Nazism), both freedom (–48) and equality (–72), not surprisingly, are the lowest possible frequencies. In fact, Hitler's keyword analysis of freedom and equality, Lenin's freedom, and Goldwater's equality demonstrate a negative use of the keywords. This means that any positive sense of freedom and equality can be substantially overwritten by negative connotations.

The numerical occurrence of the value keywords freedom and equality do discriminate. It is as Rokeach (1973, p. 170) concludes, "a theory of what politics is mainly about, namely a fundamental concern or a studied lack of concern with *equality* and *freedom*." To reiterate, Hitler ranks both equality and freedom low. Lenin ranks equality high and freedom low. The capitalists (or, perhaps more specifically, American conservatives) are high on freedom yet low on equality. The difference in the rankings within conservatism and communism samples is hardly new, as reported by Jaeger (1943) some 30 years prior to Rokeach:

> The social conflict between Liberty and Equality can be a clear issue...and...the United States and the Soviet Union...are, by their pasts, at opposite poles in this conflict, the United States combining the maximum of Liberty with the minimum of Equality, and the Soviet Union the maximum of Equality with the minimum of Liberty. (p. 123)

Returning to the near present, Wilson (2000, p. 177) reiterated that it is only the socialists who place both freedom and equality high. Value ranking derived from political documents offers strong evidence of general ideology. Rokeach (1973) says it thus:

> If we know nothing more about a person than where he stands with respect to the two distinctly political values we should be able to predict his position with respect to all major ideologues and toward the major reference persons and groups associated with the major ideologies. (p.190)

Further, he claims that, beyond these political documents, "There seems to be no reason why the present method cannot be extended to extract the values in other kinds of documents—historical, literary, biographical, and so on" (Rokeach, 1973, p. 186).

Expanding the Meaning of Democratic Discourse

Taking up Rokeach's challenge, Wilson (2000), drawing primarily from John Dewey, believed it necessary to include the two additional keywords of *community* and *democracy* to more fully capture the essence of democratic discourse. With respect to community, Dewey (1916) writes: "We live in a community in virtue of things which they have in common" (p. 4), and this "in common" then makes community possible. Such community is democratic because it is constituted by "a mode of associate living of conjoint communicated experience" (Dewey, 1916 p. 87). Within the community is the spirit of expanded participation. Davis (as cited in Pateman, 1970) writes that the theory of participatory democracy is ambitious in its attempt to educate "an entire people to the point where their intellectual, emotional, and moral capacities have reached their potential and they are joined freely and actively in a genuine community" (p. 21). There may be community, but a genuine community is possible only if constituted by its democratic nature. Thus, it is most difficult to conceive of a democratic discourse that does not contain within it a reference to a collective self that holds beliefs in common.

Concerning the addition of the keyword *democracy*, Westbrook (1991) informs us that "for Dewey, the demonstration that democracy as a form of government was the most effective means of organizing consensus and preserving stability…[and] to evaluate it simply in these instrumental terms…was to miss the more fundamental significance of democracy as an end, as an ethical ideal" (p. 41). Dewey (1888) inserted ethics into the discourse of democracy when he wrote, "Democracy is an ethical idea, the idea of a personality, with truly infinite capacities, incorporate with every man. Democracy and the one, the ultimate, ethical ideal of humanity are to my mind synonyms" (p. 248).

As Foucault (as cited in Ball, 1990) reminds us once again, different contexts give words different meanings. As Rokeach (1973) found, both conservatives and socialists are apt to use the word *democracy*, yet as they rank *equality* and *freedom* differently, *democracy* for each was clearly at variance. The singular use of any one, or even two, of the words would provide only a limited analysis of a text's democratic nature. It is only when *democracy* is used in conjunction with words such as *community*, *equality*, and *freedom* that confidence can be raised about any text's democratic nature.

Assessing Educational Reform and Literary Texts

Wilson (2000) then proceeded to further test the Rokeach "beyond the political" hypothesis by examining two educational reform texts and three literary texts. Once again, all texts were read, and the number of times the keywords *freedom*, *equality*, *community*, and *democracy* appeared was counted. The two reform texts selected were Wilford Aiken's (1942) *The Story of the Eight Year Study* and Ted Sizer's (1984) *Horace's Compromise*, which provided the framework for the Coalition of Essential Schools. Again, a discourse can be identified by the combination of the four keywords *freedom*, *equality*, *community*, and *democracy*. The more these four words and their attending categories appear in a text, the more that text represents a democratic discourse. Again, the singular use of any one, or even two, of the words would provide only a limited understanding of a text's democratic nature.

Using this standard, the results of the analysis demonstrate that the percentage of use of the words freedom, community, and democracy are favored substantially by the *Eight Year Study* with equality substantially less so but still advantageous in comparison with *Horace's Compromise*. Of the *Eight Year Study's* 11,570 words, freedom appeared 30 times (.3%), equality was present once (.009%), community 31 (.3%), and democracy 20 (.2%). For *Horace's Compromise*, the keyword counts were freedom 51 (.06%), equality 4 (.005%), community 7 (.008%), and democracy 42 (.05%). Thus, discourse of the historic *Eight Year Study* seems more democratic than the more contemporary efforts delineated in *Horace's Compromise*. This in no way suggests that *Horace's Compromise* is anti-democratic, because both texts clearly are in what can be called the tradition of liberal educational reform. A number of the principles drawn from *Horace's Compromise* are semantically close to the objectives stated in the *Eight Year Study*, yet both are virtually silent with respect to equality. As such, they reflect meaning closer to a conservative understanding of democracy rather than a social democratic ideology.

To further test the validity of using the four keywords as indicators of democratic discourse, Wilson (2000) examined three additional texts: Martin

Luther King Jr.'s speeches "Letter from a Birmingham Jail" (King, 1963) and "I Have a Dream" (Chambers, 1968) and Jonathon Kozol's *Savage Inequalities* (1991). The criterion for selecting these works was twofold: (a) reasonable persons would agree that each probably speaks to democracy in a direct way, and (b) if the latter is true, then each will contain the four words, similarly to the *Eight Year Study* and *Horace's Compromise*. Wilson (2000, p. 180) found that, of the 3,258 words in "Letter from a Birmingham Jail," freedom occurred 3 times (.9%), equality once (.03%), and democracy 25 times (.77%). "I Have a Dream," with 1,537 words, revealed freedom 20 (1.33%), equality 6 (.39%), and democracy 12 (.76%). The word community did not appear in either text. *Savage Inequalities,* with a word count of 93,200, was constituted by freedom 26 (.03%), equality 161 (.17%), community 30 (.03%), and democracy 69 (.07%).

The results of this examination demonstrate that King's rhetoric stressed the value of democracy (specifically the value category "justice") more than it did either equality or freedom. In the case of the "I Have a Dream" speech, however, freedom became the defining characteristic. Yet in both of King's texts, although freedom had higher importance than equality, freedom was cast in its positive sense of opportunity rather than in the negative sense of free from restraint, *laissez faire* form, thus linking it with equality. King's value pattern is even more democratic than either the *Eight Year Study* or *Horace's Compromise* in terms of the percentage use of the values of freedom, equality, and democracy. Interestingly, his values of equality and freedom approximate those of the democratic socialists as indicated by Rokeach in his initial work and are, in turn, discrepant from those of the communists.

This analysis suggests that although both the *Eight Year Study* and *Horace's Compromise* are closer to a conservative/capitalist ideology than they are to a democratic socialist position, the *Eight Year Study* contains a more democratic orientation than does *Horace's Compromise,* with Kozol's work falling between the two. Perhaps not surprisingly, it is only King's discourse that turns out to be the most democratic of all.

We believe that this 37-year keyword research history offers compelling evidence that it can be used to examine contemporary educational discourse specifically, in this case, that of President Obama. Just where does he stand? What do his speeches as texts tell us?

Obama's Democratic Discourse

We analyzed 71 of President Obama's speeches, of which 11 were devoted to education specifically, beginning with the 2004 speech at the Democratic National Convention to 1 year of radio addresses throughout 2009 (see Appendix B for a list of speeches). Keyword counts were recorded for each individual speech. Speech word counts were combined to calculate a total word count for all 71 speeches. Occurrence rates for each keyword category were used in combination with the total speech word count to determine the percentage and rank order of each keyword. The results of this analysis are represented in Table 5.1 (See Appendix A). The keyword categories were maintained, and included:

- Freedom (independence, free choice, liberty, autonomy, liberal)
- Equality (brotherhood, equal opportunity, egalitarian, equity)
- Community (unity, cooperation, participation, commonality, common)
- Democracy (democratic, justice, fairness, citizenship, citizen)

The key term *community* clearly predominates with 115 keywords calculated.

Democracy (67) is Obama's second-most-used keyword, with *freedom* (32) close behind and *equality* (5) a distant last. That the keyword *community* is paramount should come as no surprise, considering his tenure as a community organizer in Chicago. When compared with the findings from the Rokeach and Wilson studies, we concentrated only on the percentage of use of each keyword as the critical variable for comparison purposes.

Limiting ourselves to the data for the values of freedom and equality for the nine examples, the rank order for freedom revealed that Obama and Kozol tied with .03% keyword usage in their texts. *Horace's Compromise*, with .06%, ranked directly above them. Hitler ranked below Obama and Kozol with his last-place keyword usage in the negative range of –.20%. Not surprisingly, it was Martin Luther King Jr. who ranked number one with his keyword usage of *freedom* at 1.33%. The results seem congruent with the general perception of his historic endeavors to promote justice and fairness.

For equality, the ranking demonstrated similar scores for Obama and *Horace's Compromise*, with .005% keyword usage. Goldwater and Hitler, each scoring at negative equality percentage rates of –.04% and –.30%, respectively, rank next in line after Obama and *Horace's Compromise*. It is Lenin whose text earns the top ranking of equality keyword usage of .40%.

To determine political positioning, we then computed mean scores combining freedom with equality for each of the nine examples. The resultant democratic rank order from most to nonexistent is as follows: "I Have a Dream," "Letter from a Birmingham Jail," Lenin,[2] socialists, *Eight Year Study*, Goldwater, *Savage Inequalities*, *Horace's Compromise*, Obama, and Hitler. It would fracture common sense, if not be profoundly absurd, to conclude that Obama's, and Hitler's positions are in any sense compatible. (Recall that Hitler's use was in the negative range.) In fact, these findings, even limited to freedom and equality, demonstrate that the recent vitriolic attacks on Obama as being a communist, a socialist, and/or a fascist are indicative of widespread political ignorance. It is as if a sizable number of Americans napped through government and civics courses, assuming that they received quality instruction concerning political ideologies at all.

Because our major argument has been that the fullness of a democratic discourse depends on the total inclusion of the four keywords, we then looked at Obama's usage in comparison with those of King, *Savage Inequalities*, the *Eight Year Study*, and *Horace's Compromise*.

Obama's .22% usage of keywords places him directly above *Horace's Compromise*, which ranked last at .007%. Kozol's *Savage Inequalities* (.30%) ranked directly above Obama. It was Martin Luther King Jr. with the "I Have a Dream" speech (2.4%) who earned top ranking of democratic discourse.

These findings were then checked against Obama's usage of the keywords freedom and equality and their attending categories from his book *The Audacity of Hope*. Of 38 words found, 28 were for freedom and 10 for equality, thus a 74% advantage for freedom. These results lend additional support to our previous conclusions and reveal an acceptable consistency in the frequencies and percentages for the values of freedom and equality in comparison with Rokeach's 37-year-old study.

So, what is the meaning of all this? Considering his rank position from above, wherein the values of freedom and equality are neither extremely high nor low, with advantage more often than not going to freedom, Obama seems to fit best in the category that Rokeach (1973) labeled Middle American:

> Middle in the sense that they rank equality or freedom or both in the middle of the terminal value hierarchy. These Americans are not altogether homogeneous since

> they still vary considerably in the relative importance they place on equality and freedom. They are nonetheless moderate with respect to at least one of the two values under consideration, and it is this majority which presumably is the "silent majority."[3] (p. 193)

In Obama's case, his relative silence, that is, the lack of usage of the keywords required for political democratic discourse as we define it, seems to place him square in the middle. However, this conclusion, although necessary, is hardly sufficient. The recognition that Obama's democratic discourse is not that of a left or right political radical cannot be left to stand alone. We felt a need to go beyond the strictly political to provide insight as to what might be his governing beliefs about the ultimate aim of American education. To accomplish this task, we returned to *The Audacity of Hope* (Obama, 2006).

Obama and the Aim of Education

Although our survey was limited to *The Audacity of Hope* and is thus far from complete, we examined its pages containing the word *education* by using the index as our guide. From this search, we offer sufficient evidence that leads us to believe that we have a firm degree of confidence concerning Obama's educational ideology. From *The Audacity of Hope*, we share the words of Obama:

> Let's start with those investments that can make America more competitive in the global economy: investments in education, science and technology, and energy independence. (p. 159)

> Where knowledge determines value in the job market, where a child in Los Angeles has to compete not just with a child in Boston but also with millions of children in Bangalore and Beijing, too many of America's schools are not holding up their end of the bargain. (p. 159)

In response to a teacher lamenting the belief that so many of "these kids" can't learn, how "these kids come from tough backgrounds," or "these kids are too far behind" drives her nuts for "they're not 'these kids,' they're 'our kids.'" Obama writes: "How America's economy performs in the years to come may depend largely on how we take such wisdom to heart" (p. 163).

> And just as our government instituted free and mandatory public high schools at the dawn of the twentieth century to provide workers the skills needed for the industrial

> age, our government has to help today's workforce adjust to twenty-first-century realities. (p. 164)
>
> There is one other aspect of our educational system that merits attention—one that speaks to the heart of America's competiveness. (p. 165)
>
> New jobs created could be filled by American workers trained in new skills and a world-class education, from elementary to college. (p. 170)
>
> Education, science, and technology. Investments in these three key areas would go a long way in making America more competitive. (p. 171)
>
> And while upgrading the education levels of American workers will improve their ability to adapt to the global economy, better education alone won't necessarily protect them from growing competition. (p. 174)
>
> It's also time to redesign our schools—not just for the sake of working parents, but also to prepare our children for a more competitive world. (p. 342)

This is a language that reduces education to an economic, competitive ideology devoid of ethical concern, democratic purpose, and optimum human development so eloquently expressed by Christian Bay (1971) almost 4 decades ago. It is not a discourse of hope. It is not in the spirit of so much of his other rhetoric. Understandingly, this language came from *Audacity* and was written 2 years before his election, yet his strong support for the reworked NCLB, now morphed into the Race to the Top all seem to be of the same ideological piece probably best described as behaviorist/positivistic, as described by Wilson (1989/2010):

> The behaviorist, drawing substance from a positivistic technical rationality conceives of a world amenable to rational and scientific procedures and technique with "instrumental problem solving made vigorous by the application of scientific theory and technology" (Schon, 1983, p. 21). In this condition learning results from the efficient application of a priori discovered laws and principles and teaching becomes the execution of application science almost devoid of ethical concern. (p. 12)

In contradiction, Wilson (1989) states:

> Unlike the behaviorist ethical neutrality the progressive/critical recognizes the inescapable connection between cognition and value, between knowledge and ethics. It finds itself in essential agreement with the necessity of ethics at the core of educational discourse and accepts the socially constructed notions of knowledge, yet goes

> beyond to examine the cultural meanings embedded in any knowledge. The progressive/critical aim is to have individuals become capable of conceiving all knowledge as problematic and subject to distortion yet always open to understanding and subsequent change. (p. 12)

How could this be? Wasn't this man one of us? He did not come from a long line of politicians; he understood the struggles of "ordinary" men and women. His story gave us hope. His speeches drew us in. In his words, we perceived that change would be realized. What might explain this discrepancy, this cognitive dissonance? Although it is beyond the scope of this chapter to examine this question in depth, several possibilities come to mind. First is the historical work of Chris Argyris (1982, 1990), which offers a further hypothesis that could explain the disparity between Obama's general notions of hope and his educational ideology. As summarized by Wilson (2000), Argyris has developed and extensively tested a theory-of-action paradigm that explores the contradictions between what individuals and organizations say and do. He proposes that two kinds of theories, an espoused theory and theory-in-use, guide behavior. Espoused theories are reasons or principles that individuals use to explain their action in specific situations. Yet these theories often (more precisely, usually) do not match individual theories-in-use, the principles inferred from observation of behavior lack congruence between what people say they do and what they actually do. Argyris declares, and as sensitive observers of human nature testify, this observation, in and of itself, is not particularly new.

What Argyris has discovered is that, although people do not act in accordance with espoused theory, they do behave in congruence with their theories-in-use. At the same time, individuals remain mostly unaware of both the lack of consistency between their espoused theory and behavior and the congruence between the behavior and theories-in-use. In Obama's (2006) case, his espoused general theory of hope epitomized by his call for "The ways we can ground our politics in the notion of a common good" (p. 9) seems highly incongruent with his competitive, economic-efficiency-based, and controlling educational ideology. However, he does exhibit consistency, and his support for Race to the Top matches his reductive educational beliefs.

The second possibility is found in "Why He Has Fallen Short," a review of Jonathon Alter's book *The Promise: President Obama, Year One*. In this review, Rich (2010) cites Alter's recognition of the immense task Obama faced and his overall success rate after the first year, summed up with Alter's concluding paragraph: "Whatever happened next—however bad it got—Barack Obama was in the company of Franklin Roosevelt and Lyndon Johnson now in terms of domestic achievement, a figure of history for reasons far beyond the color of his skin" (p. 3).

Having said this, Rich does not hesitate to write: "Among those critics who are fundamentally sympathetic to Obama, explanations for his disappointing performance abound" (p. 6). Phrases such as "cautious pragmatist," "politically naïve," "subpar political skills," "surprising prolix and lackluster salesman for his own policies, and overconfidence in his ability to woo political adversaries" characterize the misgivings (p. 8). Rich further describes the trap of a "best-and-brightest arrogance" (p. 8) that began as Obama formed his transition team and continues apace today. His affection for the captains of industry and finance had little to do with their wealth or particular positioning but rather for whom he perceived them to be. Rich explains:

> But if Obama is not blinded by dollar signs, he suffers from a cultural class myopia. He's a patsy for "glittering institutions that signified great achievement for a certain class of ambitious Americans." In his books, he downplayed the more elite parts of his own resume—the prep school Punahou in Hawaii, Columbia, and Harvard—but he is nonetheless a true believer in "the idea that top-drawer professionals had gone through a fair sorting process" as he had. And so, Alter writes, he "surrounded himself with the best credentialed, most brilliant policy mandarins he could find, even if almost none of them knew anything about what it was like to work in small business, manufacturing, real estate, or other parts of the real economy." (p. 8)

To the mandarin list we add Secretary of Education Arne Duncan, who was former CEO of the Chicago Public Schools. The title of CEO reflects an economic, corporate perspective on the purpose of American education. His resume is impressive, but as far as we are able to determine, he has never actually taught or worked in a public school. The high praise he received for improving schools during his tenure in Chicago is under increasing scrutiny from a variety of sources (Anderson, 2009; Giroux & Saltman, 2008; Sharkey, 2008). Rich writes of Obama being imprisoned within his group of economic advisors. It is not a stretch to say that the following applies to his relationship with Duncan as well. The quotes are from Alter (as cited in Rich, 2010):

> "It would be increasingly difficult for him [Obama] to see beyond its borders." This "disconnection from the world," Alter concludes, was not due to ideology or the clout of special interests but was instead "the malign consequences of the American love of expertise, which, with the help of the citadels of the meritocracy, had moved from a mere culture to something approaching a cult." For all of Obama's skepticism of can't, he was "in thrall to the idea that with enough analysis, there was a 'right answer' to everything. But a right answer for whom?" (p. 10)

Duncan had the answer expressed by his behaviorist orientation. He reworked NCLB as Race to the Top. Obama's solid support for Race to the Top, when coupled with the nonappointment of Linda Darling-Hammond as Secretary of Education for whatever reason,[4] only served to increase, if not solidify, our discomfort about Obama's mostly conservative, "middle American," competitive, economic-focused educational ideology.

A Final Thought

With Obama now approaching the end of his term, there are still those who continue to question his credentials. Those who awaited a progressive, democratic approach criticize his conservative ways, whereas others accuse him of being a socialist, a communist, or a fascist. Our analysis reveals him as an articulate moderate, neither radically left nor radically right. Had it revealed him as a progressive democrat, the frequency count of keyword values would have been higher and more closely resembled the results of the *Eight Year Study* or the speeches of Martin Luther King Jr. Conversely, had the frequency count demonstrated socialist leanings, we would have seen results ranking freedom and equality in first and second place. Instead, President Obama's lack of keyword usage has placed him square in the middle; it is not that of a left or right political radical. At the end of the day, we who hoped for a "change we could believe in" are left with the reality that the words that stirred a nation are not as forward thinking as we had hoped.

In our analysis, we are aware of the dangers and unfairness of an individualistic critique grounded in the belief that there exists a leader who will save us all. There is no Superman who awaits us. Seemingly unaware of progressive alternatives, he continues to promote an educational ideology steeped heavily in the rhetoric of global competitiveness and standards-based reform. (Being against standards, testing, and the entire litany of economic efficiency of corporate reform would not be a popular stance to take.) We also take note of the political and educational climate with which he was confronted at the start of his tenure. Obama inherited a post-9/11 culture with an NCLB mind-set; his was a steep climb. However, Obama and Secretary of Education Duncan are selling this "educational reform" rhetoric as a product they believe in, ironically by using words that do not suggest progressive ideas. Promoting a democratic educational ideology would be reform in a much truer sense. Not surprisingly, this keyword analysis has revealed the "reform efforts" for what they really are: part and parcel of what Henry Giroux (2009) describes:

> The crisis I speak of in this instance is about the plight of youth as a social and political category in an age of increasing symbolic, material and institutional violence. It is a crisis rooted in society's loss of any sense of history, memory and ethical responsibility. The idea of the public good, the notion of connecting learning to social change, the idea of civic courage being infused by social justice, have been lost in an age of rabid consumerism, media-induced spectacles and short-term, high-yield financial investments. (p. 9)

Obama's educational ideology and practices are immersed in a much larger cultural environment of tension, competing claims, and power relationships. It is far beyond this chapter to explore this milieu other than to lament the immense amount of money being spent on the attack of public education by a group identified by Ravitch (2010) as a Billionaire Boys' Club that includes the Walton, Gates, Broad, Robertson, and Dell foundations. After describing how these foundations have had success in moving the educational reform agenda to one they approve of, Ravitch continues: "And so it happened that the Gates, Walton, and Broad foundations came to exercise vast influence over American education because of their strategic investments in school reform" (p. 200). Ravitch then reflects on the wisdom of this investment ideology in the context of democratic purpose:

> There is something fundamentally undemocratic about relinquishing control of the public education policy agenda to private foundations run by society's wealthiest people; when the wealthiest of these foundations are joined in common purpose, they represent an unusually powerful force that is beyond the reach of democratic institutions. These foundations, no matter how worthy and high minded, are after all, not public agencies....The foundations demand that public schools and teachers be held accountable for performance, but they themselves are accountable to no one. If their plans fail, no sanctions are leveled against them. They are bastions of unaccountable power. (pp. 200–201)

It is difficult for us to believe that both Obama and Duncan have not been influenced, if not persuaded, by foundation or corporate power when Race to the Top is placed in evidence. The discourse of democratic education is most certainly under attack by the discourse of corporate power.

Sometimes our ideological predispositions are just so fixed that we have trouble seeing the obvious. There are no enemies here. None of this is new. What surfaces is a fundamental difference in the purpose of education. Where do these ideas about education come from? As a leader of our country, there is an inherent interest in ensuring a populace poised to maintain economic security. We can understand the need to address these issues. However, is this the only purpose of our educational system?

As we worked to finalize this chapter, President Obama (2010) presented a speech to the Urban League. In his own words, he expressed the value of dialogue:

> We should all make more of an effort to discuss with one another, in a truthful and mature and responsible way, the divides that still exist—the discrimination that's still out there, the prejudices that still hold us back—a discussion that needs to take place not on cable TV, not just through a bunch of academic symposia or fancy commissions or panels, not through political posturing, but around kitchen tables, and water coolers, and church basements, and in our schools, and with our kids all across the country.
>
> If we can have that conversation in our own lives, if we can take an opportunity to learn from our imperfections and our mistakes, to grow as individuals and as a country, and if we engage in the hard work of translating words into deeds—because words are easy and deeds are hard—then I'm confident that we can move forward together and make this country a little more perfect than it was before.

These words prompt us to speak candidly to our president about the dangers of our current data-frenzied, neoliberal educational environment. We urge him to listen to the sentiments expressed by both Haim Ginott and Vicki Abeles. Ginott (1972) writes:

> This young man reminds me of a letter a teacher friend of mine received. I carry it with me. (Haim unfolds a yellowed, creased document.) I would like to share this with you:
>
> Dear Teacher,
> I am a survivor of a concentration camp. My eyes saw what no man should witness:
> Gas chambers built by learned engineers.

> Children poisoned by educated physicians.
> Infants killed by trained nurses.
> Women and babies shot and burned by high school and college graduates.
> So I am suspicious of education. My request is: help your students become more human. Your efforts must never produce learned monsters, skilled psychopaths, educated Eichmanns. Reading, writing, arithmetic are important only if they serve to make our children more human. (p. 317)

More recently, Abeles (2010), in the documentary *Race to Nowhere*, provides us with an analogy:

> Our performance-obsessed education system is "sick" and it is affecting the health and well-being of our students and teachers. When people are ill, we ask "Where does it hurt?" so we can find the remedy to "make it better." Until we ask the students and teachers who are at the core of educational health where it hurts, we will never be able to stop the contagion compromising the health and well-being—literally and figuratively—of our education system and the students and educators whose education, health and safety should thrive within the system.

Obama's (2008) victory speech inspired hope with the promise that marginalized voices would be heard because they could make a difference. We now rely on the president to keep *his* promise and listen to the voices of students and educators—voices often marginalized in discussions pertaining to education policy. President Obama, please ask the students and educators of today, "Where does it hurt?" As they answer, we hope you will apply your determination and political savvy to "make it better."

We are ethically obligated to demand an education committed to the imperatives of justice and fairness, and we believe that President Obama has the moral obligation to deliver. We close with his words from *The Audacity of Hope*:

> And in that place, I think about America and those who built it. This nation's founders, who somehow rose above petty ambitions and narrow calculations to imagine a nation unfurling across a continent. And those like Lincoln and King, who ultimately laid down their lives in the service of perfecting an imperfect union. And all the faceless, nameless men and women, slaves and soldiers and tailors and butchers, constructing lives for themselves and their children and grandchildren, brick by brick, rail by rail, calloused hand by calloused hand, to fill in the landscape of our collective dreams. It is that process I wish to be a part of. My heart is filled with love for this country. (Obama, 2006, p. 362)

collective dreams. It is that process I wish to be a part of. My heart is filled with love for this country. (Obama, 2006, p. 362)

Ours, too.

Notes

Chapter Five

1 A portion of this chapter is adapted from Wilson (2000).

2 Lenin's high ranking may come as a surprise. In his study, Rokeach employed Lenin's writings from those prior to 1917, the year of the Russian Revolution. His seizure of power and ascendency as the virtual dictator of the newly formed Soviet Union led to the Red Reign of Terror characterized by acceptance of, if not wholesale advocacy for, extreme violence, mass executions, concentration camps, forced labor policies, and induced famine that resulted in the deaths of untold thousands. Lenin's rhetoric of democratic discourse as his espoused theory clearly was not matched by his behavior (see http//econfaculty.gmu.edu/bcaplan/museum/his1g.htm; Shub, 1948). Although this contradiction raises the serious question of the relationship between values and behavior, language and action, the topic is far beyond the scope of this chapter other than in the recognition that the same conundrum applies to Obama as well as to all of us.

3 The silent majority is an unspecified large majority of people in a country or group who do not express their opinions publicly. The term was popularized (although not first used) by President Richard Nixon in a November 3, 1969, speech, in which he said, "And so tonight—to you, the great silent majority of my fellow Americans—I ask for your support." Nixon, along with many others, saw this group as being overshadowed in the media by a more vocal minority (http//en.wikipedia.org/wiki/silentmajority).

4 Ravitch (2010) writes about the prospect of Linda Darling-Hammond as Secretary of Education. "For a brief time, it appeared that the new president might pick his main campaign adviser on education, scholar Linda Darling-Hammond of Stanford University. This prospect alarmed the champions of corporate-style reform because Darling-Hammond was known as an advocate of teacher professionalism and a critic of Teach for America; the new breed of reformers thought she was too friendly with the teachers' unions." She was not a "real reformer" (pp. 21–22).

Appendix A

Table 5.1
Obama Speeches (2004–2009)
(98,615 Words)

	F	%	RO
Freedom	**32**	**.03**	**3**
Equality	**5**	**.005**	**4**
Community	**115**	**.117**	**1**
Democracy	**67**	**.07**	**2**

Note. **F=frequency, %=percentage, RO=rank order**
A list of speeches analyzed can be found in Appendix B.

Appendix B

List of Speeches

Keynote, Democratic Convention	July 27, 2004
Abraham Lincoln Library	April 20, 2005
"Literacy and Education in a 21st-Century Economy," The American Library Association	June 27, 2005
"Teaching Our Kids in a 21st-Century Economy" Center for American Progress	October 25, 2005
Civil Rights, Rosa Park's Death	October 25, 2005
Campus Progress	July 12, 2006
Vision for America	August 28, 2006
Civil Rights, MLK	November 13, 2006
National Education Association Annual Meeting	July 5, 2007
Remarks in Manning, South Carolina: "A Challenge for Our Times"	November 2, 2007
"Our Kids, Our Future," Manchester, NH	November 20, 2007
Final Primary Night	June 3, 2008
Remarks to the 80th Convention of the American Federation of Teachers. Sen. Obama spoke to the group via satellite	July 13, 2008
Acceptance speech, Democratic Convention	August 28, 2008
"A 21st-Century Education," Dayton, OH	September 9, 2008
Last night before election	November 3, 2008
Election Night Victory Speech	November 4, 2008
A More Perfect Union Speech	March 18, 2008
Inauguration	January 20, 2009
President Obama's remarks to the Hispanic Chamber of Commerce, as transcript provided by the White House	March 10, 2009
The American Presidency Project John T. Woolley & Gerhard Peters • Santa Barbara, Proclamation 8357—Education and Sharing Day, U.S.A.	April 3, 2009
Prepared Remarks of President Barack Obama, Back to School Event, Arlington, VA	September 8, 2009
2009 Weekly Radio Addresses (49)	January 24, 2009–December 24, 2009

References

Abeles, V. (Producer & Director), Congdon, J. (Director), & Attia, M. (Writer). (2010). *Race to nowhere* (documentary). Available from http://www.racetonowhere.com/film-team

Aiken, W. (1942). *The story of the eight year study.* New York: Harper and Brothers.

Anderson, N. (2009, December 28). *Education Secretary Arne Duncan's legacy as Chicago schools chief.* Available at www.washington post.com/wp-dn/content/article/2009/12/28

Argyris, C. (1982). *Reasoning, learning, and action.* San Francisco: Jossey-Bass.

———. (1990). *Overcoming organizational defenses: Facilitating organizational change.* Boston: Allyn & Bacon.

Ball, S.J. (Ed.). (1990). *Foucault and education: Disciplines and knowledge.* London: Routledge.

Bay, C. (1971). Human development and political orientation: Notes toward a science of political education. In G. Alcarion & F. Soule (Eds.), *Social psychology and political behavior* (pp. 149–182). Columbus, OH: Charles Merrill.

Brown v. Board of Education, 347 U.S. 483 (1954).

Chambers, B. (Ed.). (1968). *Chronicles of black protest.* New York: Mentor Books.

Dewey, J. (1888). The ethics of democracy. In G. Axtelle et al. (Eds.), *The early works of John Dewey* (Vol. 1, pp. 227–249). Carbondale: Southern Illinois University Press.

———. (1916). *Democracy and education.* New York: The Free Press.

Ginott, H. (1972). *Teacher and child.* New York: Macmillan.

Giroux, H. (2009, September 28). *Memories of hope in the age of disposability.* Available at www.truth-out.org/memories-hope-age-disposability63631?print

Giroux, H., & Saltman, K. (2008, December 17). *Obama's betrayal of public education? Arne Duncan and the corporate model of school.* Available at http//truth-out.org/121708R

Jaeger, M. (1943). *Liberty versus equality.* London: Thomas Nelson and Sons Ltd.

King, M. (1963). *Why we can't wait.* New York: New American Library.

Kozol, J. (1991). *Savage inequalities: Children in American schools.* New York: Crown.

National Center for Education Statistics. (2007, June). *Mapping 2005 state proficiency standards onto the NAEP scales.* Available at http://nces.ed.gov/nationsreportcard/pubs/studies/2007482.asp

Obama, B. (2004, July). Keynote address. Speech presented at the Democratic National Convention, Boston, MA.

———. (2006). *The audacity of hope.* New York: Three Rivers Press.

———. (2008). Election night victory speech. Available at http://obamaspeeches.com/E11-Barack-Obama-Election-Night-Victory-Speech-Grant-Park-Illinois-November-4-2008.htm

———. (2010). The importance of education. Remarks by president on education reform at National Urban League Centennial Conference, Washington, DC.

Pateman, C. (1970). *Participation and democratic theory.* Cambridge: Cambridge University Press.

Ravitch, D. (2010). *The death and life of the great American school system.* New York: Basic Books.

Rich, F. (2010, August 19). Why has he fallen short? [Review of *The promise: President Obama, year one*, by J. Alter]. *The New York Review of Books*. Available at http://www.nybooks.com/articles/2010/aug/19/why-has-he-fallen-short/?pagination=false&printpage=true

Rokeach, M. (1973). *The nature of human value.* New York: The Free Press.

Sharkey, J. (2008, December 17). *Duncan's school "reform" sham.* Available at http://dissidentvoice.org/2008/12/duncans-school-"reform"-sham/

Shub, D. (1948). *Lenin* (special abridged edition). New York: New American Library.

Sizer, T. (1984) *Horace's compromise: The dilemma of the American high school.* Boston: Houghton Mifflin Company.

Westbrook, R. (1991). *John Dewey and American democracy.* Ithaca, NY: Cornell University Press.

Williams, R. (1983). *Key words: A vocabulary of culture and society.* New York: Oxford University Press.

Wilson, T. (1989). *Design and educational ideologies: Who designs what for whom and how.* (ERIC Document Reproduction Services No. ED313016). Revised (2010) Chapman University.

———. (2000). Comparing discourses: Democratic values, the coalition of essential schools and the eight year study. In M. Leicester, C. Modgil, & S. Modgil (Eds.), *Education, culture and values: Vol. VI. Political education and citizenship* (pp. 173–182). London: Falmer Press.

❖ PART THREE ❖

DEMOCRACY AS THE FOUNDATION OF POLICY

❖ CHAPTER SIX ❖

Federalism, Education, and Citizenship in an Era of Democratic Deliberation

Brian L. Fife

President Barack Obama's basic philosophical premise about the proper role of the federal government in the economy and education is encompassed in his own words:

> Hamilton's and Lincoln's basic insight—that the resources and power of the national government can facilitate, rather than supplant, a vibrant free market—has continued to be one of the cornerstones of both Republican and Democratic policies at every stage of America's development. The Hoover Dam, the Tennessee Valley Authority, the interstate highway system, the Internet, the Human Genome Project—time and again, government investment has helped pave the way for an explosion in economic activity. And through the creation of a system of public schools and institutions of higher education, as well as programs like the GI Bill that made a college education available to millions, government has helped to provide individuals the tools to adapt and innovate in a climate of constant technological change. (Obama, 2006, pp. 152–153)

In his book *The Audacity of Hope*, published 2 years before he was elected president of the United States, Obama articulates a political vision where citizens and elected officials alike seek to find common ground in order to address many vexing public policy challenges. Instead of focusing on divisions between and among groups, he suggests a pragmatic approach to policymaking in which diverse groups of people identify where consensus can be achieved as a starting point toward the creation and implementation of more effective public policies. Yet unlike some politicians, the president maintains that both government and the citizenry have a joint responsibility to improve the lives of American citizens. He does not envision a passive population that simply reacts to policies after they are made. In fact, he contends that the optimum manner in which to address the needs of the people is to embrace the republican ideals of the framers of the Constitution, as applied to the early 21st century, and shed rigid orthodoxy and ideology:

> The outlines of Madison's constitutional architecture are so familiar that even schoolchildren can recite them; not only rule of law and representative government, not just a bill of rights, but also the separation of the national government into three coequal branches, a bicameral Congress, and a concept of federalism that preserved authority in state governments, all of it designed to diffuse power, check factions, balance interests, and prevent tyranny by either the few or the many. Moreover, our history has vindicated one of the Founders' central insights: that republican self-government could actually work better in a large and diverse society, where, in Hamilton's words, the "jarring of parties" and differences of opinion could "promote deliberation and circumspection." As with our understanding of the Declaration, we debate the details of constitutional construction; we may object to Congress's abuse of expanded commerce clause powers to the detriment of the states, or to the erosion of Congress's power to declare war. But we are confident in the fundamental soundness of the Founders' blueprints and the democratic house that resulted. Conservative or liberal, we are all constitutionalists. (Obama, 2006, pp. 87–88)

In short, Barack Obama is a person of faith who embraces the notion that democratic deliberation can yield positive and tangible policy results. Implicit in this theoretical notion is an educated citizenry. An educated and compassionate population is likely to pursue progressive reform and utilize a general ethos of reasonableness and common sense. In this manner, Barack Obama is not touting a new philosophy of education. He is, in fact, restating a rather old philosophy that is still largely intact. Horace Mann, the 19th-century common school reformer, stated in 1848:

> Such, then, in a religious point of view, is the Massachusetts system of Common Schools. Reverently, it recognizes and affirms the sovereign rights of the Creator; sedulously and sacredly it guards the religious rights of the creature; while it seeks to remove all hinderances, and to supply all furtherances to a filial and paternal communion between man and his Maker. In a social and political sense, it is a *Free* school system. It knows no distinction of rich and poor, of bond and free, or between those who, in the imperfect light of this world, are seeking, through different avenues, to reach the gate of heaven. Without money and without price, it throws open its doors, and spreads the table of its bounty, for all the children of the State. Like the sun, it shines, not only upon the good, but upon the evil, that they may become good; and, like the rain, its blessings descend, not only upon the just, but upon the unjust, that their injustice may depart from them and be known no more. (cited in Cremin, 1957, pp. 111–112)

A compelling theme reverberates throughout *The Audacity of Hope*. It is a simple one, really, but we need to collectively remind ourselves of it in a periodic manner. If we do not support the status quo on a given issue, we have the wherewithal to change it. A policy reality today does not need to perpetuate if it is harmful in nature. Progressive reformers have embraced this notion throughout America's brief history as a nation. This has quite clearly been demonstrated in the case of voting, and a reflection of past accomplishments by democratic reformers will follow so as to suggest, with little subtlety, that there is ample room for reform at the present time.

Philadelphia Convention of 1787

The framers of the U.S. Constitution ordained that voting in the United States is an exercise in federalism. As stipulated in Article I, Section 4:

> The Times, Places and Manner of holding Elections for Senators and Representatives, shall be prescribed in each State by the Legislature thereof; but the Congress may at any time by Law make or alter such Regulations.

While the framers permitted state officials to create the rules governing their elections, members of Congress may intervene as they deem necessary. In 1845, for example, Congress created a national election day for the first time in U.S. history (3 U.S.C. 1). Prior to then, states were permitted to conduct their presidential elections any time during a 34-day period (before the first Wednesday in December) pursuant to a federal law passed on March 1, 1792 (1 Stat. 239). Electing U.S. representatives on Election Day in every even-numbered year was established in 1875 (2 U.S.C. 7). In 1914, members of Congress determined that U.S. senators would be selected on this date as well (2 U.S.C. 1).

The United States, as devised by the framers of the Constitution, is a federal republic. When the framers deliberated from May through September in 1787 (see Farrand, 1966), one reality at the time was the sheer existence of 13 separate states. Consistent with the states' rights ideology as it pertains to elections, as well as pragmatism in terms of traveling, state officials had significant discretion in devising rules governing their respective electoral systems. This practice continues in contemporary society. A comparison of a number of state laws governing voting and elections captures a great deal of diversity between and among the states (Fife, 2010).

Voter Registration Laws in the American States[1]

In 1972, the U.S. Supreme Court justices made their decision in the *Dunn v. Blumstein* case. In this case, a Tennessee law required a 1-year residence in the state and a 3-month residence in a county as a precondition for voting. A controversy occurred when James Blumstein moved to Tennessee on June 12, 1970, to commence employment as an assistant professor of law at Vanderbilt University in Nashville. On July 1, he attempted to register to vote in the August and November elections that year. The county registrar refused to register him because he did not meet the preconditions for voting under Tennessee's law. Through this case, the justices determined that registration up to 30 days before the election is reasonable in order to give officials time to prepare for the election. Although computer technology has changed dramatically since 1972, this standard is still in operation today (*Dunn v. Blumstein*, 1972).

Table 6.1
In-Person State Voter Registration Laws for General Election Dates (2009)

Voter Registration Law	States with This Law	*N*
No registration required	North Dakota	1
Same day registration	Idaho, Iowa, Maine, Minnesota, Montana, New Hampshire, Wisconsin, and Wyoming	8
6 days before election	Vermont	1
7 days before election	Connecticut	1
10 days before election	Alabama	1
11 days before election	Nebraska	1
15 days before election	California, Kansas, South Dakota, Utah, and Washington	5

Table 6.1 Continued on next page

Table 6.1 (Continued)

20 days before election	Delaware and Massachusetts	2
21 days before election	Maryland, Nevada, New Jersey, Oregon, and West Virginia	5
25 days before election	New York, North Carolina, and Oklahoma	3
27 days before election	Missouri	1
28 days before election	Illinois, Kentucky, and New Mexico	3
29 days before election	Arizona, Colorado, Florida, Indiana, and Virginia	5
30 days before election	Alaska, Arkansas, District of Columbia, Georgia, Hawaii, Louisiana, Michigan, Mississippi, Ohio, Pennsylvania, Rhode Island,[1] South Carolina, Tennessee, and Texas	14

1 Rhode Island General Law 17-1-3 allows a citizen who has missed the voter registration deadline to vote for president and vice president only at the local Board of Canvassers on election day.

Source: League of Women Voters Education Fund. 2010. *Voting in Your State.* Retrieved January 20, 2010, from http://www.vote411.org/bystate.php.

As illustrated in Table 6.1, 31 of 51 state laws (the District of Columbia is included because it has electors in presidential elections) require a waiting period for voter registration of at least 3 weeks. Fourteen state laws require the full 30 days permitted by the Supreme Court justices back in 1972 (the year that Republican Richard Nixon was reelected as president over Democratic candidate George McGovern). Another eight states have waiting periods of 28 or 29 days. Contrast the laws in these states to those in Idaho, Iowa, Maine, Minnesota, Montana, New Hampshire, Wisconsin, and Wyoming, where same-day registration exists (i.e., citizens can register and then vote on Election Day). North Dakota is the only state in the union that does not require voluntary registration, meaning that all residents are eligible to vote when they turn 18 years of age. In short, at least on this one issue and undoubtedly several others as well (Fife, 2010), some states have laws that make voting much easier for their citizens without increasing the risk of fraudulent voting.

It should be understood that voter registration lists serve two basic functions in the American democracy. First, the voter registration requirement helps to ensure that only those citizens who are eligible participate in the electoral process and that each citizen gets exactly one vote. This purpose is constructive and equitable. The other purpose is not legitimate, and it is unjust in a democracy. Voter registration has been used for more than a century by those who control the administration of elections to make it cumbersome for their political opponents to exercise the right to vote. In simple terms, it has been used as a barrier to prevent certain groups from fully exercising the franchise in this republic.

The States' Rights Ideology

Political conservatives throughout history have generally believed that the national government, particularly the U.S. Congress, is limited in its ability to engage in public policymaking. Based in part on the context of the times in question, a consistent theme has persisted throughout the history of the American republic. Under a narrow interpretation of congressional power via Article I, Section 8, conservatives have long maintained that Congress has a limited mandate under the federal Constitution and that state governments have the authority to address all powers not explicitly granted to Congress. This is based on an interpretation of the meaning of the Tenth Amendment. Throughout U.S. history, however, many have rebuked the states' rights ideology. States' rights advocates, such as Patrick Henry, opposed ratification of the Constitution after the Philadelphia Convention because he felt that the new Congress would be too powerful compared with the states (Mayer, 1991). The authors of *The Federalist Papers*, Alexander Hamilton, James Madison, and John Jay, triumphed on the ratification issue, however, because many Americans understood that a stable democracy could only be achieved if Congress had more authority than it did under America's first constitution, the Articles of Confederation and Perpetual Union. A few decades later, the issue of a national bank rekindled the passions of those who believed that a more prosperous republic required a strong national government and those who believed in the doctrine of states' rights.

The members of Congress originally chartered the Bank of the United States in 1791 at the urging of Secretary of the Treasury Alexander Hamilton. It was rechartered in 1816. In early 1818, the Maryland state legislators imposed a tax on all banks operating in their state that were not chartered by them. Only one such bank existed: the Baltimore branch of the Bank of the United States. The cashier of the Baltimore branch refused to pay the state tax when approached on several occasions by state officials. Consequently, Maryland officials took their dispute to a state court (*McCulloch v. Maryland*, 1819).

A primary point of contention between the officials representing the national government and those from Maryland had to do with constitutional interpretation. Maryland officials believed that the Bank of the United States was unconstitutional because the power to create a national banking system was not specifically assigned to Congress under Article I, Section 8 of the Constitution. From the perspective of agents of the national government, Congress created the Bank of the United States in pursuance of its constitutional powers. The last section of Article I, Section 8 includes the power of Congress:

> To make all Laws which shall be necessary and proper for carrying into Execution the foregoing Powers, and all other Powers vested by this Constitution in the Government of the United States, or in any Department or Officer thereof.

The cashier of the Baltimore branch maintained that Congress had the explicit power to tax as well as coin and borrow money under the Constitution. These powers would not come to fruition without a national banking system. Chief Justice Marshall and the other justices on the Supreme Court agreed (*McCulloch v. Maryland*, 1819). In his opinion, the chief justice determined that Congress had not only enumerated powers under the Constitution but also implied powers as well under the "necessary and proper" clause. He opined that:

> If any one proposition could command the universal assent of mankind, we might expect it would be this—that the government of the Union, though limited in its powers, is supreme within its sphere of action. This would seem to result, necessarily, from its nature. It is the government of all; its powers are delegated by all; it rep-

> resents all, and acts for all. Though any one state may be willing to control its operations, no state is willing to allow others to control them. The nation, on those subjects on which it can act, must necessarily bind its component parts. But this question is not left to mere reason: the people have, in express terms, decided it, by saying "this constitution, and the laws of the United States, which shall be made in pursuance thereof," "shall be the supreme law of the land," and by requiring that the members of the state legislatures, and the officers of the executive and judicial departments of the states, shall take the oath of fidelity to it. The government of the United States, then, though limited in its powers, is supreme; and its laws, when made in pursuance of the constitution, form the supreme law of the land, "anything in the constitution or laws of any state to the contrary notwithstanding." (*McCulloch v. Maryland*, 1819)

Thus, the justices nullified the Maryland state tax because they determined that no state, under the Constitution, had the legal authority to tax the national government.

Almost a century later, President Theodore Roosevelt explained his view of federalism when discussing presidential power. He viewed himself as an ardent nationalist when progressive issues were at stake:

> [L]ittle permanent good can be done by any party which worships the State's rights fetish or which fails to regard the State, like the county or municipality, as merely a convenient unit for local self-government, while in all National matters, of importance to the whole people, the Nation is to be supreme over State, county, and town alike. (Roosevelt, 1914, p. 366)

The needs of the undifferentiated people of the United States supersede the perceived interests of any specific state. Under the federal Constitution, the national government and the 50 state governments are not equal. Federal law is supreme over state law; this reality is important both in education and many other policy areas.

In the summer of 1948, a young mayor of Minneapolis issued a bold declaration regarding the doctrine of states' rights at the Democratic National Convention (American Rhetoric, 2009). Mayor Hubert Humphrey (he would later serve as a senator and vice president, and he was the Democratic nominee for president in 1968, losing a close election to Richard Nixon) exclaimed:

> My friends, to those who say that we are rushing this issue of civil rights, I say to them we are 172 years late. To those who say that this civil-rights program is an infringement on states' rights, I say this: The time has arrived in America for the

> Democratic Party to get out of the shadow of states' rights and to walk forthrightly into the bright sunshine of human rights. People—human beings—this is the issue of the 20th century. People of all kinds—all sorts of people—and these people are looking to America for leadership, and they're looking to America for precept and example. (American Rhetoric, 2009)

The great irony involved in Mayor Humphrey's declaration in 1948 is that the Constitution was amended in 1868, following the Civil War, with the Fourteenth Amendment:[2]

> All persons born or naturalized in the United States, and subject to the jurisdiction thereof, are citizens of the United States and of the state wherein they reside. No state shall make or enforce any law which shall abridge the privileges or immunities of citizens of the United States; nor shall any state deprive any person of life, liberty, or property, without due process of law; nor deny to any person within its jurisdiction the equal protection of the laws.

All citizens are intrinsically equal under the federal Constitution. Thus, the treatment of citizens is not a debate in federalism under the Constitution first and foremost; it is a matter of constitutional law. State governments are not empowered to treat citizens in an unequal manner, because the Fourteenth Amendment precludes such behavior. Yet for any constitutional guarantee to be meaningful, it has to be enforced. This is precisely why Mayor Humphrey implored his fellow Democrats after World War II to cease focusing on civil rights as a federalism question rather than a constitutional mandate and moral imperative. Today, this same debate reverberates across the nation when certain state legislatures pass laws, state supreme court judges issue rulings, and/or popular referendums disallow same-sex couples from getting married within their borders. Is this an issue that should properly be decided by each and every state, or are citizens supposed to be treated equally under the Fourteenth Amendment? Lessons from U.S. history suggest that the contemporary focus on federalism when it comes to gay marriage is ill advised and downright contrary to the Constitution.

The Importance of Theory in Education Policy

One of the most important aspects of politics and education is theory. Plausible theoretical ideas are absolutely essential in the pursuit of more scientific knowledge about given public policy issues. A prolific student of law, Oliver Wendell Holmes Jr. made the following statement in the late 19th century:

> Theory is the most important part of the dogma of the law, as the architect is the most important man who takes part in the building of a house. The most important improvements in the last twenty-five years are improvements in theory. It is not to be feared as unpractical, for, to the competent, it simply means going to the bottom of the subject. For the incompetent, it sometimes is true, as has been said, that an interest in general ideas means an absence of particular knowledge. I remember in army days reading of a youth who, being examined for the lowest grade and being asked a question about squadron drill, answered that he never had considered the evolutions of less than ten thousand men. But the weak and foolish must be left to their folly. The danger is that the able and practical minded should look with indifference or distrust upon ideas the connection of which with their business is remote. (Holmes, 1897, pp. 477–478)

Thus, in order for President Obama, or any other public official or interested citizen, to reform public education, prudent ideas are the most fundamental entities required to participate in a substantive exercise that will render meaningful change in the education sector.

The Importance of History in Education Policy

Before proceeding to a more detailed discussion of K–12 public education in the United States, it is important to emphasize the study of history in this venue as well as any other. Oftentimes contemporary citizens perceive that certain challenges are somehow novel and unique to them and their time period. Although technology is obviously ever changing, many of our educational challenges and debates have been in existence for generations. The actors in the arena may change, but the issues are fairly constant, and much can be learned from the trials, tribulations, successes, and failures of the past. When ascertaining the importance of history in the legal field, Justice Holmes quipped that:

> At present, in very many cases, if we want to know why a rule of law has taken its particular shape, and more or less if we want to know why it exists at all, we go to tradition. We follow it into the Year Books, and perhaps beyond them to the customs

> of the Salin Franks, and somewhere in the past, in the German forests, in the needs of the Norman kings, in the assumptions of a dominant class, in the absence of generalized ideas, we find out the practical motive for what now best is justified by the mere fact of its acceptance and that men are accustomed to it. The rational study of law is still to a large extent the study of history. History must be a part of the study, because without it we cannot know the precise scope of rules which it is our business to know. It is a part of the rational study, because it is a first step toward an enlightened skepticism, that is, towards a deliberate reconsideration of the worth of those rules. (Holmes, 1897, p. 469)

Education laws and policies that do not serve a reasonable purpose and are reflective of past attitudes, beliefs, and perhaps even inequality toward some students are ripe for reconsideration. In the education policy process, laws—even prudent ones that serve their stated objectives and serve the greater public interest—require constant revision. With this in mind, it is time to reflect on the involvement of the federal government in public K–12 education in both historical and contemporary contexts.

Overview of Federal Involvement in Public K–12 Education

Public education at the K–12 level has been historically defined and perceived as a state and local responsibility in the United States. The structure of education finance illustrates this substantive reality. In the 2009–2010 academic year, 89.5% of the costs for elementary and secondary education came from state, local, and private sources. The federal contribution of 10.5% emanated primarily from the U.S. Department of Education but also from other federal agencies, including the U.S. Department of Health and Human Services (Head Start program) and the U.S. Department of Agriculture (School Lunch program) (U.S. Department of Education, 2010). Yet there has been federal involvement in public education throughout American history, even before the U.S. Constitution was ratified and took effect in 1789.

According to researchers at the Center on Education Policy, officials representing the federal government became involved in education for four major reasons:

- to promote democracy,
- to ensure equality of educational opportunity,
- to enhance national productivity, and
- to strengthen national defense. (Center on Education Policy, 1999, p. 3)

Professor Joel Spring (2008) has presented similar observations in his historical overview of the American school.

Promoting Democracy

Democracy is not by definition a passive entity. It requires a well-educated and proactive citizenry in order to flourish as a system. Educated citizens are inclined to acquire civic values and a sense of common national identity (Center on Education Policy, 1999). When this republic began, it did not take reformers long to understand the premise that it was in the national interest to establish a system of public education. Clearly, Horace Mann understood this reality in the 19th century. The common school experience, from his perspective, would result in less societal conflict and more human compassion for fellow citizens, and ultimately would render good Democrats and Republicans alike (Center on Education Policy, 1999; Cremin, 1957).

Agents of the Congress of the Confederation created the Northwest Ordinance of 1787 (the same year as the Philadelphia Convention). The unsettled territory of the United States was divided into townships, each consisting of 36 sections measuring one square mile. The ordinance authors determined that one of every six sections should be rented out and the proceeds used to support public education. Thus, federal law had the effect of encouraging the establishment of public schools even before the U.S. Constitution was ratified (Center on Education Policy, 1999).

Particularly since the publication of *A Nation at Risk* in 1983 (National Commission on Excellence in Education, 1983), federal legislators have attempted to assist state and local officials in the important task of raising student achievement. This objective was emphasized during a decade-long movement to reform public education, which culminated in Goals 2000: Educate America Act (Public Law 103-227, 1994). Enhancing student achievement and reducing the gap between and among students was an objective of the No Child Left Behind (NCLB) Act (Public Law 107-110, 2002), although interpretations of the primary substantive intent of the law would obviously be varied in nature (Meier & Wood, 2004).

Ensuring Educational Opportunity

During the Civil Rights Movement of the 1950s and 1960s, federal officials were primarily focused on the right of every citizen to participate equitably in public education. In some instances, federal intervention has come by way of Congress, by actions within the executive branch, or through the federal courts. The landmark achievement during the mid-20th century was *Brown v. Board of Education of Topeka, Kansas* in 1954. Laws or policies promoting racial segregation in the public schools were rendered invalid by a unanimous Supreme Court through the decision authored by Chief Justice Earl Warren.

Later, federal officials determined that many poor and disadvantaged children were not receiving an adequate education. As part of his War on Poverty, President Lyndon Johnson convinced his colleagues in Congress to pass a major cornerstone in education policy, the Elementary and Secondary Education Act (ESEA) of 1965 (Public Law 89-10, 1965). The ESEA was later reauthorized and is now known as the NCLB law. Members of Congress provided aid to states and school districts in this act to improve education for children from low-income families and to meet other critical education needs (Center on Education Policy, 1999).

Enhancing National Productivity

As early as the mid-19th century, officials at the federal level began to take action designed to prepare citizens for the workforce and to expand their opportunities beyond high school. When state leaders began to establish public colleges and universities, their counterparts at the federal level passed the Morrill Act of 1862 (U.S. National Archives and Records Administration, 2010a). As a result of this act, grants of federal land were made available to states to establish "land-grant colleges" offering agricultural and engineering courses. Many institutions benefitted from this act, including Cornell University, the Massachusetts Institute of Technology, Pennsylvania State University, Purdue University, and the University of California (Center on Education Policy, 1999).

During the early part of the 20th century, it became apparent to many that the United States lacked trained workers to fill new jobs in manufacturing and agriculture. Accordingly, federal funds were appropriated through a series of measures in order to encourage communities to establish vocational education. In addition, during and especially after World War II, federal programs designed to expand access to higher education were created (Center on Education Policy, 1999). The most recognizable program, undoubtedly, is the Servicemen's Readjustment Act of 1944, otherwise known as the G.I. Bill (U.S. National Archives and Records Administration, 2010b). Another important program traces back to President Johnson's Great Society, when the Higher Education Act of 1965 was signed into law (Public Law 89-329, 1965). Pell Grants initially started as Basic Educational Opportunity Grants (BEOGs) in 1972, when the Higher Education Act of 1965 was reauthorized. BEOGs were later renamed Pell Grants after Senator Claiborne Pell (D–Rhode Island), who was the chief advocate for providing indigent students with financial assistance so they could pursue their higher education objectives (Public Law 110-315, 2008).

Strengthening National Defense

Federal officials have attempted to strengthen national defense through education for decades. In 1958, in response to the Soviet launching of the satellite *Sputnik* a year earlier, members of Congress passed the National Defense Education Act (NDEA) (Spring, 2008; Public Law 85-864, 1958). Clearly, U.S. officials wanted to ensure that highly trained, skilled professionals would be available so that the United States could compete with the Soviet Union in scientific and highly technical fields. Consequently, the NDEA included provisions for loans to college students; funds to assist in improving science, mathematics, and foreign-language training in elementary and secondary schools; graduate fellowships; funds to assist in foreign-language training and area studies in higher education; and funds to enhance vocational-technical training (U.S. Department of Education, 2010).

In a consistent manner since the end of World War II, federal officials have attempted to promote mathematics and science, not only during the Cold War era, but in the post-9/11 period as well. Policymakers have operated on a similar paradigm for decades: the national security needs of the United States can be addressed, in part, through public education. This phenomenon is evidenced by the existence of the National Science Foundation, which has offered programs for 60 years, designed, in part, to improve student performance in science and mathematics and to enhance teacher skills in these areas (Center on Education Policy, 1999; National Science Foundation, 2010).

The Federal Government and Education Reform

In order to reform public education in the common school tradition, Americans should not abdicate their commitment to public schools, because if they do, they will have less accountability over the educational enterprise. The assault on the common school ideology with regard to choice, privatization, and even charter schools (Spring, 2008) will have harmful consequences for our democratic republic if resources are shifted away from the public sector and toward the private sector. Americans will have less accountability over a policy issue that was designed to be mostly public in nature (Cremin, 1957).

The federal government should have a role in reforming public education. The doctrine of states' rights should not be embraced in any meaningful way, because federal officials have always had a role in public education, even before the republic established under the Constitution began in 1789 (i.e., the Northwest Ordinance of 1787). Although the federal role has typically been a small one compared to state and local governments, particularly in financial terms, politicians at the national level should do anything they can to assist their colleagues at the state and local levels in delivering the most effective public educational systems possible. Thus, the federal role has historically been—and should continue to be—a supportive one; interventions are justified to pursue lofty national goals. Congress has a broad mandate under Article I of the federal Constitution to promote the common good. The members of the national legislature have a moral responsibility to do so as well.

In today's terms, to understand the federal role in education, it is truly necessary for all citizens to understand the federal budget in terms of mandatory and discretionary spending, in both legal and pragmatic terms. President Obama recently proposed his budget for fiscal year 2011.[3] His plan seeks congressional approval to spend $3.834 trillion during fiscal year 2011; his request for the U.S. Department of Education is $49.7 billion, or 1.3% of the total budget (Office of Management and Budget, 2010). Bear in mind that overall federal funding of education (K 12 and higher education) is typically about 2% of the entire budget (Center on Budget and Policy Priorities, 2009).

There are important budget realities, however. About 60% of the budget is already spent from one year to the next in real terms. Currently, entitlement programs such as Social Security, Medicare, and Medicaid, as well as other safety-net programs, coupled with interest payments on the total national debt, cover three-fifths of the budget. The remaining 40% of the budget is discretionary in nature but not in reality. National defense and security matters are considered discretionary spending items in terms of the federal budgetary process. Currently, about 20% of the total budget is allocated for defense and security. The remaining 20% of the budget covers everything else funded by the federal government, including education (Center on Budget and Policy Priorities, 2009). In the arena of American politics, federal lawmakers and U.S. presidents are constrained by what they can and cannot do in terms of educational priorities. Yet there is still a role for the federal government in education, and it is not an incidental one.

President Obama seemingly shares this conception regarding the role of the federal government in education:

> If we want an innovation economy, one that generates more Googles each year, then we have to invest in our future innovators—by doubling federal funding of basic research over the next five years, training one hundred thousand more engineers and scientists over the next four years, or providing new research grants to the most outstanding early-career researchers in the country. The total price tag for maintaining our scientific and technological edge comes out to approximately $42 billion over five years—real money, to be sure, but just 15 percent of the most recent federal highway bill. In other words, we can afford to do what needs to be done. What's missing is not money, but a national sense of urgency. (Obama, 2006, pp. 166–167)

The philosophical premise articulated by the president has deep roots in the American education tradition. It is a vision of federalism with regard to education policy that suggests that there is a discernible link between education and economic development. Although we must guard against undue business influence in public education (Spring, 2008), it would be difficult to sustain any premise that suggests that the United States will compete more effectively in the complex global economy by deemphasizing education. It is highly counterintuitive.

Ironically, citizens could play a more effective role in education by educating themselves about the realities of education financing, understanding the history of education and the common school movement, coming to terms with the politics of education, and becoming more engaged in public affairs in general. Americans' reticent approach to politics is fairly well documented; it is not a significant priority for many, and although all citizens, adults and children alike, are affected by public policymaking, many are not very proactive when it comes to citizenship. American voter turnout is among the lowest in the democratic world.

Table 6.2
Voter Turnout in U.S. Presidential Elections, 1932–2008
(Percentage of Voting Age Population Who Voted)

Presidential Election	Voter Turnout (%)
1932	52.6
1936	56.9
1940	58.8
1944	56.1
1948	51.1
1952	61.6
1956	59.3
1960	62.8
1964	61.4
1968	60.7
1972	55.1
1976	53.6
1980	52.8
1984	53.3
1988	50.3
1992	55.2
1996	49.0
2000	50.3
2004	55.6
2008	56.8

Sources: U.S. Census Bureau. 2009. *The 2009 Statistical Abstract. Elections: Voting-Age Population and Voter Participation.* Retrieved August 10, 2009, from http://www.census.gov/

compendia/statab/tables/09s0402.pdf (1932–2004); and U.S. Elections Project. 2009. *2008 General Election Turnout Rates.* Retrieved May 21, 2009, from http://elections.gmu.edu/voter_turnout.htm (2008).

In presidential election years, voter turnout in the United States (see Table 6.2) is typically between 50% and 55% of all adults. Turnout in many other free nations in analogous elections is typically in the 70th percentile or higher (Fife, 2010). The path to reform in the United States, especially during the Progressive Era, was based on a significant amount of activism on the part of the populace; a passive citizenry is one that generally does not succeed in altering the status quo in a meaningful manner. The stakes are comparatively high during presidential election years because, in addition to the presidency, all seats in the U.S. House of Representatives and one third of all U.S. Senate seats are contested, as well as state and local offices. Yet almost half the population does not even bother to vote. There is ample room for reform on this issue as well.

The Need for Effective Federal Intervention in Education

Federal intervention is still needed in public education (Center on Education Policy, 1999). Yet when federal officials do engage in education policymaking, they must have reasonable goals and objectives, and the intervention in question must be prudent and—most important—effective. An important starting point, however, has to be the debunking of myths and stereotypes about the current state of education in America. There is much to celebrate in terms of education today, and too little of this substance is communicated to the people. Also, there is very little coverage of what is "right" in education today in the mass media.[4] Americans are constantly bombarded with the recurring allegations that schools are failing, teachers are not working diligently enough, the school environment is unsafe, and a host of other accusations. In reality, there are many positive features to today's public schools (Center on Education Policy, 2005), although by definition there will always be room to reform any human public policy endeavor. A public policy that is in dire need of reform, although well intentioned in many ways, is NCLB (Meier & Wood, 2004). Here is a case where federal intervention may have been warranted, but the manner in which it was accomplished was ill advised and downright harmful.

NCLB is based on a premise that is quite difficult to oppose. As one practitioner noted:

> Who could object to a law that promises no child left behind when it comes to our schools? After all, isn't this the great promise of our public school system—that all children, regardless of race, socioeconomic status, gender, creed, color or disability will have equal access to an education that allows them to enjoy the freedoms and exercise the responsibilities of citizenship in our democracy? (Meier & Wood, 2004, p. vii)

Most would intuitively agree with the premise that all children deserve a quality education. Yet NCLB has been in effect for almost 10 years, and many dispute its relative effectiveness. Although much can be debated about this law (Meier & Wood, 2004), the issue of federalism generally does not garner much debate, given the history of public education as being primarily a state and local question. The old paradigm that state and local officials are best equipped to identify students' educational needs warrants reexamination. Most agree that reforms are needed and justified. In part, there is at least tacit recognition that some state and local leaders have failed to address the policy needs of their students, or where subnational leaders require federal assistance, history is replete with examples of federal intervention with, in many instances, tangible results. The NCLB law, however, was predicated on a theoretical assumption that is of dubious value today and will not promote the cause of education reform in an era where America must improve its educational standards so as to compete in a more competitive global economy.

The original NCLB Act is flawed in multitudinous ways (Meier & Wood, 2004). In terms of testing, one researcher noted the shortcomings of the law's requirements:

> The one-size-fits-all assessment requirements—annual testing in reading and math and periodic testing in science—and the accountability provisions attached to them are rigid, harmful, and ultimately unworkable. They will promote bad educational practices and deform curricula in significant ways. In the end, they will lower, not raise, standards for most students. For example, the assessment requirements will lead to further devaluing of non-tested subjects like social studies, music, and art. NCLB focuses on large-scale testing, which is a poor tool for diagnosing individual students' needs and for assessing higher-order learning. The provisions of the law are turning large numbers of schools, particularly those serving low-income children, into test-prep programs. The testing regime punishes the teachers who choose to work in the nation's underresourced schools and fosters the inaccurate view that most of the nation's public schools are failing. (Neill, 2004, p. 103)

A fundamental starting point in analyzing NCLB is federalism. Reflective of the states' rights history of public education, the NCLB architects determined that each state would have its own instrument to determine which students were passing and failing various subjects. There is no national standard, so what can be deduced, for example, if Americans read that 45% of seventh graders in Indiana passed the Hoosier math examination while 68% of students in seventh grade in Maine passed the Pine Tree state's math examination? In reality, no comparative conclusion can reasonably be ascertained from this information, because the students did not take the same instrument, and it may be that the students' schools have different curricular standards. This type of comparison has been evidenced for years when it comes to SAT scores. If state X has the highest SAT averages in the nation, but only 55% of all graduating seniors take the exam, compared to state Y, which has average SAT scores about 30 points below state X, but 82% of all graduating seniors take the exam, which state has higher achievers? Is the comparison fair in that scores are higher in state X, but it appears that officials in state Y are more proactive in encouraging graduating seniors to take the exam so that presumably more students matriculate in a bachelor's program? All of this understates another important reality about NCLB. Many educators believe that a single test, regardless of who creates it, is not a reliable indicator of a student's progress in her or his educational career. Social science and education researchers typically advocate multiple measures so as to garner a more comprehensive overview of a child's educational achievement.

When federal policymakers created NCLB, they avoided at least two significant issues in federalism—undoubtedly, in part, for political reasons. First, federal officials mandated that their counterparts at the state level would have to engage in more testing, presumably to hold education leaders and teachers accountable. But they did not hold the states to a specific standard, so each state has its own benchmarks, and it is virtually impossible to conduct meaningful comparisons. Second, federal policymakers avoided, at least in 2001–2002, a deliberative and substantive discussion about national standards, even if such standards were voluntary in nature. This was a mistake, and, at the present time, an effort to draft common standards for high school graduates is being conducted by the National Governors Association (*The New York Times*, February 1, 2010). An earnest dialogue about a national curriculum for public school students, one that is substantive and challenging and may be based on existing state models, is long overdue.

The most important requirement in the NCLB law is that all students must be proficient (according to state definitions) in reading, math, and science by 2014. This is a laudable objective. In a utopian world, such proficiency would be possible. But this lofty standard will not enhance education quality; it will actually lower it (Meier & Wood, 2004; Neill, 2004). Perhaps the starkest reality, however, is that policymakers have seemingly ignored an unpleasant truth that is perhaps one of the most disturbing features of contemporary American life: almost 20% of children in the United States today live in poverty (U.S. Census Bureau, 2010). This is the highest rate in the industrialized world, and it is based on the federal poverty guideline, which is currently $22,050 for a family of four living in the 48 contiguous states and the District of Columbia (U.S. Department of Health and Human Services, 2010). Researchers have known, at least since the Moynihan Report in 1965, that poverty affects educational achievement (U.S. Department of Labor, March, 1965). There is no suggestion that children from impoverished backgrounds cannot learn and succeed in academics; the point is simply that social class affects standardized test performance.

President Obama and the Cause of Education Reform

As of this writing, President Obama and leaders in the U.S. Department of Education are seeking to change many aspects of NCLB, including the elimination of the law's 2014 proficiency deadline (*The New York Times*, February 1, 2010). Negotiations with members of Congress may continue into the foreseeable future. If an accord between the two primary institutions can be achieved, it is crucial that it be one that is supportive of public education and the common school ideal and does not promote the cause of privatization. If a key benchmark of a democratic nation is accountability to the people, then education needs to be defined largely as a public good where federal officials earnestly seek to assist their peers at the subnational levels and promote excellence in education and provide the necessary vision and resources to ensure that children, regardless of their current status, receive a quality education so that they can pursue their own professional aspirations. This is the kind of hope and optimism that all adults should provide America's children.

Notes

Chapter Six

1 The diversity between and among the states in terms of political culture is captured by Daniel J. Elazar (1984).

2 U.S. senators approved the Fourteenth Amendment on June 8, 1866, by a vote of 33 to 11. Members of the U.S. House of Representatives approved the same measure on June 13, 1866, by a vote of 120 to 32. It was ratified by the requisite number of states on July 28, 1868 (Library of Congress, 2010).

3 The fiscal year for the federal government runs from October 1 to September 30. Thus, fiscal year 2011 begins October 1, 2010, and ends on September 30, 2011 (see Office of Management and Budget, 2010).

4 Review the 24 indicators of the "latest good news about American education" in Center on Education (2005).

References

American Rhetoric. (2009). *Hubert Humphrey: Democratic National Convention Address, July 14, 1948*. Retrieved December 19, 2009, from http://www.americanrhetoric.com/huberthumphrey1948dnc.html.

Brown v. Board of Education of Topeka, Kansas, 347 U.S. 483 (1954).

Center on Budget and Policy Priorities. (2009, December 4). *Policy basics: Where do our tax dollars go*? Retrieved February 5, 2010, from http://www.cbpp.org/files/4-14-08tax.pdf.

Center on Education Policy. (1999). *A brief history of the federal role in education: Why it began and why it's still needed.* (ERIC Document 438335)

———. (2005, August). *Do you know....The latest good news about American education*? Retrieved February 5, 2010, from http://www cep-dc.org/index.cfm?

Cremin, L. (Ed.). (1957). *The republic and the school: Horace Mann on the education of free men*. New York: Teachers College Press.

Dunn v. Blumstein, 405 U.S. 330 (1972).

Elazar, D. J. (1984). *American federalism: A view from the states* (3rd ed.). New York: Harper & Row.

Farrand, M. (Ed.). (1966). *The records of the federal convention of 1787* (Vols. I–IV). New Haven, CT: Yale University Press.

Fife, B. (2010). *Reforming the electoral process in America: Toward more democracy in the twenty-first century*. Santa Barbara, CA: ABC-CLIO.

Holmes, O.W., Jr. (1897). The path of the law. *Harvard Law Review*, *10*(8), 457 478.

League of Women Voters Education Fund. (2010). *Voting in your state*. Retrieved January 20, 2010, from http://www.vote411.org/bystate.php

Library of Congress. (2010). *Primary documents in American history: 14th amendment*. Retrieved January 30, 2010, from http://www.loc.gov/rr/program/bib/ourdocs/14th amendment.html

Mayer, H. (1991). *A son of thunder: Patrick Henry and the American republic*. Charlottesville: University Press of Virginia.

McCulloch v. Maryland, 17 U.S. 316 (1819).

Meier, D., & Wood, G. (Eds.). (2004). *Many children left behind: How the No Child Left Behind Act is damaging our children and our schools*. Boston: Beacon Press.

Mendez, B.E. (November 23, 2009). The obama generation revisited, The Nation. 289, 17, p 13.

National Commission on Excellence in Education. (1983, April). *A nation at risk: The imperative for educational reform*. Retrieved February 3, 2010, from http://www2.ed.gov/pubs/NatAtRisk/index.html

National Science Foundation. (2010). *National Science Foundation history*. Retrieved February 4, 2010, from http://www.nsf.gov/about/history

Neill, M. (2004). Leaving no child behind: Overhauling NCLB. In D. Meier & G. Wood (Eds.), *Many children left behind: How the No Child Left Behind Act is damaging our children and our schools* (pp. 101–119). Boston: Beacon Press.

The New York Times. (2010, February 1). Obama to seek sweeping change in "No Child" law. Retrieved February 9, 2010, from http://www.nytimes.com/2010/02/01/education/01child.html?scp=1&sq=nclb%20reform%20obama&st=cse

Obama, B. (2006). *The audacity of hope: Thoughts on reclaiming the American dream*. New York: Crown Publishers.

Office of Management and Budget. (2010). *Budget of the U.S. government: Fiscal year 2011*. Retrieved February 4, 2010, from http://www.whitehouse.gov/omb/budget/fy2011/assets/budget.pdf

Public Law 85-864. (1958, September 2). National Defense Education Act of 1958. Retrieved February 4, 2010, from http://www.constitution.org/uslaw/sal/072_statutes_at_large.pdf

Public Law 89-10. (1965, April 11). Elementary and Secondary Education Act of 1965. Retrieved February 4, 2010, from http://www.eric.ed.gov/PDFS/ED017539.pdf

Public Law 89-329. (1965, November 8). Higher Education Act of 1965. Retrieved May 11, 2011, from http://ftp.resource.org/gao.gov/89-329/00004C57.pdf

Public Law 103-227. (1994, March 31). Goals 2000: Educate America Act. Retrieved February 3, 2010, from http://www2.ed.gov/legislation/GOALS2000/TheAct/index.html

Public Law 107-110. (2002, January 8) No Child Left Behind Act of 2001. Retrieved February 3, 2010, from http://www2.ed.gov/policy/elsec/leg/esea02/107-110.pdf

Public Law 110-315. (2008, August 14). Higher Education Opportunity Act. Retrieved February 3, 2010, from http://www2.ed.gov/policy/highered/leg/hea08/index.html

Roosevelt, T. (1914). *Theodore Roosevelt: An autobiography*. New York: Macmillan.

Spring, J. (2008). *The American school: From the Puritans to No Child Left Behind* (7th ed.). Boston: McGraw-Hill.

U.S. Census Bureau. (2009). *The 2009 statistical abstract. Elections: Voting-age population and voter participation*. Retrieved August 10, 2009, from http://www.census.gov/compendia/statab/tables/09s0402.pdf

———. (2010). *Poverty: 2008 highlights*. Retrieved February 9, 2010, from http://www.census.gov/hhes/www/poverty/poverty08/pov08hi.html

U.S. Department of Education. (2010). *The federal role in education*. Retrieved February 1, 2010, from http://www2.ed.gov/print/about/overview/fed/role.html

U.S. Department of Health and Human Services. (2010). *The 2009 HHS poverty guidelines*. Retrieved February 9, 2010, from http://aspe.hhs.gov/poverty/09poverty.shtml

U.S. Department of Labor. (1965, March). *The Negro family: The case for national action*. Retrieved February 9, 2010, from http://www.dol.gov/oasam/programs/history/webidrpage.htm

U.S. Elections Project. (2009). *2008 general election turnout rates*. Retrieved May 21, 2009, from http://elections.gmu.edu/voter_turnout.htm

U.S. National Archives and Records Administration. (2010a). Morrill Act (Public Law 37-

108, July 2, 1862). Retrieved February 3, 2010, from http://www.ourdocuments.gov/doc.php?doc=33

———. (2010b). Servicemen's Readjustment Act (Public Law 78-346, June 22, 1944). Retrieved February 3, 2010, from http://www.ourdocuments.gov/doc.php?doc=76

❖ CHAPTER SEVEN ❖

A New American Social Compact: Finding the Space and Compassion to Discover Common Purposes

Jane A. Grant

As we near the end of the first decade of the 21st century, Americans appear adrift, unsettled, and divided, with little sense of common purpose. Fourteen years ago, political theorist Michael Sandel (1996) described the "twin anxieties" that seemed to be making Americans uncomfortable with their nation and themselves. Sandel noted the "fear that, individually and collectively, we are losing control of the forces that govern our lives" (p. 3). There was also the deep concern that "the moral fabric of community is unraveling." Today, those anxieties remain.

In at least the classical understanding of the polis associated with a "civic republic," the public sphere is where citizens gather to grapple with critical problems and deliberate about the moral and ethical implications of the solutions they choose (Grant, 2008). However, with the changed governing ethos that emerged in the United States in the late 1930s and early 1940s, which Sandel (1996) has called a "procedural republic" orientation, Americans spend less time engaged with each other in pursuit of the common good. Contemporary "public spaces" are instead focused on personal, lifestyle, commercial, sensationalistic, and highly polarizing matters. As a result, the polity, which includes the beliefs, practices, and institutions that characterize the approach to governance in a nation, is now primarily associated with the formal institutions of government in the United States. Americans in 2010 express little confidence that these institutions, especially at the national level, are capable of dealing with the most pressing issues facing the nation (Pew Research Center, 2010).

In 1957, "73% of Americans trusted the government to do what is right just about always or most of the time." In 2010, only 22% of Americans expressed such confidence (Pew Research Center, 2010). Although these numbers have gone up and down over the last 50 years, during the past decade they have been in consistent decline. Public trust in government stood at around 55% after the attacks of September 11, 2001; by October 2008, only 17% of Americans "trusted the federal government to do what is right" (Pew Research Center, 2010). Why Americans presently have such a low estimation of their government's efficacy may be the result of two phenomena: one longer term, the other more proximate. The larger historical trend is the transformation of the American polity from a civic republican ethos to a procedural republican one (Grant, 2008; Sandel, 1996); this will be discussed more fully later. The other condition is the contemporary struggle, especially in the last 60 years, to define the rights and the values that should comprise the present-day procedural orientation. The conflicts over how the citizens of this nation now understand its essential purposes are also examined.

Historical Transformation of the American Polity

A civic republic is the older conception of a democratic society, associated with the early Greek city-states and Roman republics (Grant, 2003; Mansbridge, 1983; Sandel, 1996). Sandel (1996) and Bellah (1992) believe this was the dominant influence on the ethos of the United States during its founding. A civic republic focuses on producing virtuous citizens who engage directly in their own governance. It is concerned with "formative" values and institutions that shape the character of citizens to prepare them to direct their futures (Sandel, 1996). The key limitation of this orientation, at least as it was practiced in Greece, Rome, and the first century and a third of America's existence, was its exclusivity. When the U.S. Constitution was ratified in 1788, voting was a right that only white males and, in some states, only property-owning males enjoyed. Native Americans, African Americans,[1] and women were legally barred from the franchise during different periods of a 130-year span following the Constitution's ratification (Burns, 1982).

Moreover, this nation, with its early civic republican focus on virtue, condoned, for the first 74 years of its existence, the institution of slavery, allowing for the most immoral of conditions in a society that dedicated itself to the proposition that "all men are created equal" (The Declaration of Independence, 1776).

Yet like many other things in America, the promise of such ideals held critical influence, even when the ideals failed to be realized. The paradox of Jefferson, a slaveholder, articulating a vision of the independent farmer, who, because he owned his own land, was thus capable of participating in meaningful self-governance, is palpable (Sandel, 1996). Yet it was Jefferson's ideas that also influenced Lincoln, who in the end was critical to the passage of the Thirteenth Amendment to the Constitution banning slavery (Sandel, 1996; The Constitution of the United States, 1787). Both Jefferson and Lincoln endorsed the notion that "we are free only insofar as we exercise our capacity to deliberate about the common good, and participate in [the] public life" (Sandel, 1996, p. 26). Both saw this as central to a democratic polity.

Sandel notes that the Progressive Era, from about 1870 to 1920, represented the last best effort to combine the ideals of a civic republic concerned with the common good and the attempt to also expand the polity to include previously excluded groups. During that 50-year period, initiatives were undertaken to improve both the conditions under which citizens lived in a newly industrializing society as well as their rights. These included attempts to establish maximum hours and minimum wages for workers; efforts to improve public education, public health, and the environment in burgeoning urban centers; a series of national programs to protect public lands and resources; and the passage of the Nineteenth Amendment in 1920, which gave women the right to vote (Grant, 2008).

Yet in the aftermath of World War I and the end of the Progressive Era, there was a backlash against what some viewed as "intrusive" government efforts and the moralizing tendencies that surrounded them. When Franklin Delano Roosevelt became president in 1933, the country was faced with large and deep-seated problems that he believed required national solutions. Although in the early years of his administration he initiated programs that were reminiscent of the Progressive Era in which he was raised and whose ideals he revered, by the mid to late 1930s, Roosevelt began to rely on a different logic to justify his efforts to put the nation back to work; provide for the old, sick, and infirm; and build the nation's infrastructure (Sandel, 1996). His turn to a different justification for these national undertakings was in part an attempt to deal with the continued backlash, particularly among Republicans, against what was seen as a federal government that was too big and too costly. It was also a realization that the nation, now larger and more diverse than ever, would have difficulty in agreeing on a set of shared values that all could strongly endorse. Roosevelt turned to Keynesian fiscal policy as a means by which he could focus on the good of American society, by ensuring that citizens would have what they needed to lead productive lives without having the government define what was good for each citizen. Through deficit spending, redistributive social programs, and a growing economy, individuals would have the opportunities to decide for themselves what constituted a "good life." Keynesian fiscal policy, combined with key U.S. Supreme Court decisions, especially beginning in the 1940s, began to exemplify the logic of the contemporary procedural republic that focused on the autonomy of individuals and the "neutrality" of government (Grant, 2008; Sandel, 1996).

Sandel (1996) argues that, as the philosophy of the procedural republic began to unfold in the late 1930s and early 1940s, and certainly by the middle of the 20th century, almost all Americans could be considered "liberals." These "contemporary liberals" (whether Democrats, Republicans, or Independents) broadly supported the notion that the best society is one built on guaranteeing individuals the freedom to make the most important decisions concerning their own lives; this orientation is directly linked to the philosophy of liberalism that emerged in the 18th and 19th centuries. In the contemporary procedural republic, however, significant differences have emerged over the role that government should play in such a society. "Libertarian" liberals (Sandel, 1996), who both then and now are largely associated with the Republican Party, argue for limited government. The less government intervention in the economy, the better; the more individuals have the "liberty" to determine what to do with their incomes, the better. "Egalitarian" liberals, who both then and now are largely associated with the Democratic Party, also strongly support individual rights and autonomy. However, they additionally see the need for government intervention in the society and economy to ensure fairness: rights need to be protected equally, and imbalances of power in a market economy need to be corrected (Sandel, 1996). To some extent, these differences were muted in the period of dynamic economic growth that followed the end of World War II. Yet the differential focus on "growth" versus "distributive justice" (Sandel, 1996) would become profound in the late 1950s, 1960s, and 1970s. During this period, new social and political movements on the left emerged to question the ethos of postwar

America, whereas a strong counter reaction on the right also made its appearance.

The Strains in the Contemporary Procedural Republic[2]

There are two significant sources of conflict in the contemporary procedural republic (Sandel, 1996). The first is the appropriate role for government in modern society, shaped largely by the debate between libertarian and egalitarian liberals (Sandel, 1996). Egalitarian liberals were the dominant force in American politics from the time of the New Deal through the end of the Johnson administration in the late 1960s. Libertarian liberals emerged as a counterforce in American politics beginning in the late 1960s and then moved into prominence during the presidencies of Ronald Reagan in the 1980s and George W. Bush from 2000 to 2008 (Sandel, 1996). The other source of contention, both within and between these two orientations, is about what values and ethics are needed for a good society, questions the procedural republic seeks to avoid.

Although the movements of the 1960s have often been described as efforts to expand the rights of previously excluded groups, and they certainly were this, they also raised significant questions about what kind of nation we were and what kind of nation we wanted to be. The Civil Rights Movement, the Women's Movement, the Anti-Vietnam War Movement, the Environmental Movement, and later the Gay Rights Movement and the Disability Rights Movement focused on issues of equality and inclusion, tolerance and respect, but also on our obligations to each other, the direction and purposes of the economy, our relationships with other nations, and our stewardship of the biosphere. Since the 1930s, the Democratic Party has been a big-tent party, with many groups that share both common and conflicting perspectives. The center/progressive/radical left points on the political spectrum associated with the Democratic Party can be roughly divided into three contingents, with varying degrees of concurrence with "egalitarian liberalism" (Sandel, 1996).

Near the center of the overall political spectrum, and at the right end of the Democratic Party coalition, would be those individuals and groups who, by and large, see a need for government intervention in the society and economy to protect rights and to promote fairness; however, they prefer that this be done gradually. They prefer less expansive government initiatives, decreased government spending, and a focus on deficit reduction and economic growth. They adhere to the liberal notion of having individuals decide for themselves what constitutes a good life while the government remains neutral on such matters. Yet these "centrists" understand that government has a role to play to ensure a more fair and equal society.

The left-of-center group in the Democratic Party, the "progressive" contingent, desires a more expanded role for the government in the society and the economy, moving closer to the egalitarian ideal of many Western European countries. Although progressives accept the reality of capitalism, they believe that governing structures have a responsibility to build a more secure and sustainable future for citizens. Progressives also have a comprehensive orientation to expanding equality and human rights.

Finally, on the more radical end of this spectrum, many of whose adherents may not even identify as Democrats, are those who argue for significant structural changes to the economy and the society. Included here are groups pressing for dismantling the military-industrial war complex and restraining the power of multinational corporations; an ecocentric understanding of the biosphere that would put species' survival needs ahead of human acquisitive interests and economic growth; and increased freedom from the "grid" so that individuals are less dependent on the larger society, moving toward a more decentralized and, in some cases, an anarchic utopia.

There are clearly overlapping perspectives among these three groups; however, tactics and strategies may distinguish them. The center-progressive groups work within the existing legislative, administrative, judicial, political, economic, and cultural frameworks to bring about change. At the far left end of this spectrum, some individuals and groups, but certainly not all, may condone the use of violence in the attempt to radically change social, economic, and political structures. The anti-globalization or the animal/earth liberation movements provide possible examples of this (Grant, 2008).

In response to the upheavals set in motion by the movements of the 1960s and 1970s, a powerful backlash emerged from more traditional, conservative, libertarian, and radical right orientations of the American polity. Of those groups on the right end of the political continuum, at least four contingents can be identified. The first represents the modern remnants of the Jeffersonian-Lincoln civic ideal; they would be situated closest to the center of the political spectrum, although clearly on the right. These individuals believe in the power of local community and the ideal of participation; however, for these modern civic republicans, participation is focused on civil society and the variety of religious, voluntary, and charitable groups that make up that sector. They support limited national government, the sharing of power with state governments, and a strong military. Ronald Reagan clearly appealed to this group as he made the case for a vision of America anchored in small communities (Grant, 2008).

A second group, which Reagan also appealed to, is comprised of those who want to restrict the government's role in the economy and society. Some members of this contingent, particularly since the 1990s Gingrich revolution, have actually taken a radical turn to the right in their efforts to privatize what had previously been accepted parts of the public sector: Social Security, public education, prisons and highway systems, and even defense and military functions. For these conservatives, the "free" market is seen as the solution to all individual and societal problems (Grant, 2008), and Ronald Reagan's belief in supply-side economics is mirrored in the contemporary mantra of lowering taxes and decreasing government spending. Some economic conservatives are social liberals or even libertarian; they believe the government should remain neutral on a wide variety of choices that individuals can and should make for themselves.

The third and fourth groups on the conservative end of the political spectrum were key supporters of George W. Bush, although their influence was felt as early as the 1980s. They include religious conservatives who want to replace the "neutrality" of the public sphere with a set of values based on a narrow and fundamentalist interpretation of Christian theology. They have focused on "family" values as the basis on which a new and more moral society should be reconstructed. Then there are the groups that have supported aggressive and triumphalist foreign policies, in some cases motivated by deeply held religious beliefs. These individuals, many of whom surrounded George W. Bush as he sought justifications to invade Iraq in 2003, are referred to as the "neoconservatives" or "neo-cons" (Grant, 2008).

As with the groups on the center-left end of the political spectrum, the groups on the center-right end may have overlapping perspectives. In the current political climate, the moderate span on this continuum seems to be shrinking while other activists have moved further to the right, whether in terms of adherence to a fundamentalist Christian theology, support for radical privatization goals, or pressure for increased global military interventions. As with the extreme left, there are individuals on the right who hope to achieve their goals through the use of violence, including those who support the ideology and actions of local militias, white supremacy groups, and survivalist and separatist organizations. As with the center-left end of the spectrum, it is likely that the more extreme members of these groups do not consider themselves Republicans, although the kind of heated and offensive language used at some rallies in support of John McCain and Sarah Palin in the 2008 election indicate that at least some of these individuals find common cause with the Republicans (Shear & Bacon, 2008).

I believe the slide in the public's perception of the efficacy of the federal government in the last 10 years is linked to deep disappointments and frustrations by some groups within both the conservative/Republican and progressive/Democratic ends of the political spectrum. Although religious conservatives and neoconservatives remained loyal to George W. Bush until the end, his presidency was a deep disappointment to the fiscal conservatives who saw the size and scope of government and federal deficits expand enormously under his leadership from 2001 to 2008 (Ruffing & Horney, 2010). The more civic-oriented groups among Republicans, I suspect, may have felt betrayed by what they came to view as an unnecessary and costly war and the vast and dangerous expansion of executive power during the Bush presidency (Grant, 2008).

Additionally, both the mismanagement of the war in Iraq and Hurricane Katrina could not have added to Americans' belief in the efficacy of their government. Some of those who called themselves independents in the 2008 elections may in fact have been disaffected Republicans who fell into these latter two groups. Of course, it may be many of these individuals who have provided the energy fueling the Tea Party movement. This movement against government, against defining shared purposes, sparked to a significant degree by economic dislocation and, to some extent, prejudice and misinformation, is lashing out at both the legacy of the Bush administration and the attempts of the Obama administration to provide answers to national problems (Zernike & Thee-Brenan, 2010).

In contrast, the Obama presidency, although bringing together a vast array of groups that wanted "change," has also been a disappointment to those in the progressive camp of the Democratic Party.[3] The Obama administration, of course, has faced enormous problems not of its own making: a spectacular financial collapse, involvement in two ongoing wars whose attempts at nation-building have not been noticeably successful, and the explosion of the Deepwater Horizon rig in the Gulf of Mexico on April 20, 2010, leading to a potentially significant environmental disaster. President Obama, unlike Franklin Roosevelt, has been unable to articulate a vision for his presidency that brings disparate groups together for what might be defined as a shared purpose. Instead, he has been slow in responding to emerging political problems, hesitant about exerting leadership, and willing to compromise to the point where the results become less than noteworthy and satisfying to few. So, where does the nation turn when some feel the government is doing too much, others feel it is not doing enough, and the vast majority find themselves facing a weakened economy, national drift, and a nation seemingly without purpose?

A New American Social Compact

Background

I have previously written about the need to develop a new American social compact for the 21st century (Grant, 2008). This new compact would seek to combine the best attributes of the civic republic with those of the procedural republic (Sandel, 1996). The compact would be defined by a new *civic procedural ethos*. Most social contract theories, although not all, are linked to the 18th and 19th centuries and the emergence of modern liberalism (Grant, 2008). A social contract meant that citizens would give up some liberties to establish a set of governing institutions that could then protect the agreed-on civil and political rights of all citizens. Government was to be limited in the modern liberal orientation as emphasis was placed on individuals determining the best way to lead their own lives. As noted previously, this perspective provided the foundation for the contemporary procedural republic, as described by Sandel (1996). In contrast, the earlier civic republican orientation (Sandel, 1996) depended on a shared communal ethos and the pursuit of common purposes, within which a limited set of rights was protected. Citizens were expected to participate together to cast their future; they understood and acknowledged their dependence on each other. The contemporary procedural republic (Sandel, 1996), instead, is premised on a loosely constructed ethos that surrounds a much more extensive set of rights. The public sphere is to remain "neutral" on what comprises a "good life" (Sandel, 1996); those choices are to be made by individuals. The dilemma here, and the dilemma of the contemporary procedural republic, is whether we can or should avoid talking about values, with each other, in the public sphere, and whether we can or should ignore how extensively we rely on each other, other nations, and other species for our very survival (Grant, 2008; Sandel, 1996).

Although the social contract that emerged in the 18th and early 19th centuries focused largely on civil and political rights, by the late 19th century it also began to include a new set of social rights. Among these were universal or near-universal access to public education, national health insurance, and public pension systems, as well as the development of workplace health and safety laws and environmental protection statutes (Grant, 2008). The modern social contract, therefore, can be used to understand not only our rights but the obligations we may have to others. However, I have chosen to use the term *social compact* to describe a broader conception that encompasses the rights that individuals have in a fair and equitable society, as well as a set of principles that affirm our obligations to each other or any other significant entity designated by the polity. In the attempt to merge the best of the civic and procedural republics, I have called the ethos of this new social compact a *civic procedural* one. Civil, political, and social rights would be honored for their significance and intrinsic validity, while civic and shared purposes would also be central to the compact. The principles defining our obligations would be developed through discussions in our representative institutions, along with newly created venues for democratic deliberation. In addition, the emergence of new social and political movements and the election of accountable and ethical leaders would be crucial to the new compact (Grant, 2008).

The Significance of Democratic Deliberation

Democratic deliberation is central to a new social compact. It can, if done properly, address some aspects of the fears that Sandel (1996) argues characterize the times in which we live: feelings of not being in control of the significant forces shaping our lives and drifting in a normless land. Historian Tony Judt (2010), in the months before his death, addressed the deep-seated apprehensions that mark our lives in contemporary America. He observed:

> We have entered an age of insecurity—economic insecurity, physical insecurity, political insecurity….Insecurity breeds fear. And fear—fear of change, fear of decline, fear of strangers and an unfamiliar world—is eroding the trust and interdependence on which civil societies rest. (pp. 8–9)

If implemented properly, public deliberative opportunities could allow exploration of what may be a critical source of this insecurity: the fear that we can no longer rely on each other for help or assistance and that we are all essentially on our own. Deliberative forums may help to clarify misunderstandings or misinformation in policy disputes. Beyond that, effective deliberation could allow us to address or at least acknowledge our values and to better see how these values are linked to our policy positions. In some cases, face-to-face deliberation can also help us to discover those values and interests that may be broadly shared or potentially useful in policy decisions (Grant, 2003).

Rawls (1997) notes that when we discuss our values in public, we need to express those values in terms that others can understand and even accept, even though the values we hold may derive from our own particular "reasonable comprehensive" doctrines. Thus, Rawls (1997) states:

> What public reason asks is that citizens be able to explain their vote to one another in terms of a reasonable balance of public political values, it being understood by everyone that of course the plurality of reasonable comprehensive doctrines held by citizens is thought by them to provide further and often transcendent backing for those values. (p. 116)

A civic republic is one in which citizens participate directly in their own governance, and the purpose of that participation is to seek the common good. In developing a civic procedural ethos, deliberation may be central to allowing us to discuss significant issues within an ethical or a value-oriented framework. There have been many proposals for how deliberative opportunities could be built into contemporary American society, from Dahl's (1985) notion of the mini-populus to Ackerman and Fishkin's (2004) *Deliberation Day*, to Ethan Leib's (2004) idea for developing a new "popular branch of government." Several things would have to be present for deliberative democracy to be useful for developing a new social compact.

First, it is necessary for there to be a certain level of respect among the participants in any deliberative opportunity.[4] This respect may need to be generated from training sessions before the deliberation takes place or from the presence of professional facilitators during deliberations. Second, the deliberative arena must provide access to a wide range of information and perspectives that participants require as they deliberate on a subject. With both increased respect for one another and increased access to information, those involved in a deliberation have the possibility to move beyond their given preferences to see issues from a new perspective. Jon Elster (1997) notes that deliberative democracy does not use the market logic that sees "politics [as] the aggregation of given preferences" but instead views politics as "the transformation of preferences through rational discussion" (p. 4).

Third, it must be linked to or provide input for decision making in our formal institutions of government. Joshua Cohen (1997) observes: "At the heart of the institutionalization of the deliberative procedure is the existence of arenas in which citizens can propose issues for the political agenda and participate in debate about those issues" (p. 85).

Well-developed venues for democratic deliberation can provide opportunities for citizens to deal with each other respectfully in a public setting. They provide a possibility for citizens to get beyond their own, sometimes narrow and self-interested view of issues, to something that may move them to consider or even embrace a common purpose. In a public space, with due respect, adequate supports, sufficient information, and links to formal decision-making institutions, citizens may be able to draw on a sense of compassion and empathy to actually care about others. Biologist Franz De Waal (2009) observes that

> biology is usually called upon to justify a society based on selfish principles, but we should never forget that it has produced the glue that holds communities together. This glue is the same for us as for many other animals. Being in tune with others, coordinating activities, and caring for those in need is not restricted to our species. Human empathy has the backing of a long evolutionary history. (p. x)

Even if a deliberative opportunity fails to draw any general consensus from participants, it can at least clarify how our values lead to certain policy positions or political stances. This may be helpful to citizens as well as to our elected leaders. Public deliberation that is linked to formal decision-making processes may offer "public" opinion, which is both more representative and informed (Dahl, 1985) than the "subjectless communication" Habermas describes (as cited in Bohman & Rehg, 1997) as pervading our senses in contemporary society. The answers to our political, social, and economic problems should not come from those who shout the loudest, are less than adequately informed, promote intolerance and hatred, or have the most resources to saturate us with their positions. Democratic deliberation may help to foster more accountability from our elected leaders and therefore lead to some greater degree of control over our governing institutions than is presently the case in our "thin" democracy (Barber, 1984).

Deliberation and Public Education

Democratic deliberation and public education are linked in two key senses. The first derives from the civic purposes of public schools. From the beginning in the United States, education has been seen as necessary to produce citizens capable of governing themselves. It is in the public space of a school that ideas are discussed, debated, and broadly clarified among a student body diverse in backgrounds, beliefs, religious orientations, and socioeconomic status. As Brian Fife (Chapter 6 in this volume) observes:

> When this republic began, it did not take reformers long to understand the premise that it was in the national interest to establish a system of public education. Clearly, Horace Mann understood this reality in the 19th century. The common school experience, from his perspective, would result in less societal conflict and more human compassion for fellow citizens, and ultimately would render good Democrats and Republicans alike. (p. 128)

Of course historians such as James MacGregor Burns (1982) have noted that U.S. public schools have long served seemingly contradictory purposes, emphasizing civic involvement and social equality, on the one hand, while being a conduit for differential achievement and uneven upward mobility, on the other. Yet some contemporary analysts of public education have become alarmed at the extent to which the latter aims appear to have become the central purposes of contemporary American education. Instead of concern with civic values, shared purposes, the common good, and our obligations to others, U.S. educational policy has moved dramatically into a realm focused on individualized success and material objectives, where what is most valued is that which can be measured. Evaluations of individuals and schools are built around a set of instrumental and economic indicators that rely on the logic of market efficiency. Frederick Taylor's "scientific management" (as cited in Kline, 2007) may no longer be a model just for the industrial workplace; the same rationale of standardization, limited autonomy, and production utilities is now the basis on which teachers and students are judged (Dillon, 2010). Little attention or care is paid to what happens outside the classroom, either in the complex psychological, social, and economic environments from which students come or to the kind of society we would like to have and the vital roles students might play within it. Henry Giroux (2010) notes the reason "traditional" public education now poses such a threat in the contemporary context is that

> it associates teaching and learning with civic values, civic courage, and a respect for the common good—a position decidedly at odds with the unbridled individualism, privatized discourse, excessive competition, hyper militarized masculinity and corporate values that now drive educational policy and practice. (p. 5)

Although public school classrooms could provide the space where the skills needed for informed and active citizens, who can contribute to the "commonwealth" of the nation, are nurtured and a place where learning in its most basic and exciting sense takes place, the contemporary public school is now off on a different track. Educational policy is so focused on the need to routinize learning that teachers

> are now forced to simply implement predetermined instructional procedures and standardized content, at best; and, at worst, put their imaginative powers on hold while using precious classroom time to teach students how to master the skill of test taking. (Giroux, 2010, p. 1)

The other way in which democratic discourse is essential to public education is through the kind of discussions that should be taking placing in the larger society about the role, purposes of, and resources needed for effective public education in our society. Although changes in the United States since the 1970s have made funding for public education somewhat more equally distributed (Corcoran, Romer, & Rosenthal, 2008), we are failing as a society to adequately invest in public education:

> Our initial look at how education finance since *Serrano* has played out across the country suggests that there have been achievements in equity. But, when viewed from the perspective of the entire system of public education, progress may well have come at the expense of total resources devoted to education, particularly to average or somewhat below-average income districts. (Corcoran et al., 2008, p. 73)

We currently do not have the kinds of forums, linked to decision-making institutions, in which citizens, with respect for each other and with adequate information, in a public place, could deliberate about the value of public education and the kinds of investments we as a society should be making. Critical decisions about our children are now being made either in private by families who, wanting the best for their children and with the resources to do it, move to districts with "better schools" (which invest more in their teachers, students, and educational resources) or send their children to private schools. For poorer families, members of minority groups, and those with a range of disabilities, opportunities are dependent on economically driven paradigms that equate scores on standardized tests with successful learning. Teachers are then punished for low student performance, whether the learners in a particular class have English as a second language, sit in overcrowded and underequipped classrooms, or have to deal with a variety of social, psychological, and economic problems each day, all of which remain outside of the classroom teacher's control. Little attention is paid to longer-term outcomes or what the real goals of education policy should be. As a result of these trends in national educational policies, our nation is more divided and less empathetic, increasingly focused on individual gain and less willing to share the burdens and costs, as well as the benefits, of living and working together in a worthwhile society.

Social and Political Movements and Accountable Leaders

Besides deliberation, social movements have often been linked to critical changes in our nation's ethos, values, policies, and practices. This can be seen in the Abolition Movement in the early to mid-19th century; the Progressive Movement at the end of the 19th and the beginning of the 20th centuries; and the Workers' Rights Movement in the 1930s. It can also be seen in political and social movements that have emerged since the late 1950s, including the Civil Rights Movement, the Anti-Vietnam War Movement, the Women's Movement, the Environmental Movement, the Gay Rights Movement, and the Disability Rights Movement. Advocates for critical changes have to make their case to both their fellow citizens and to their elected leaders; sometimes after long periods of sustained conflict and struggle, after the motives of those seeking changes have been impugned, after they have sacrificed much in their lives to achieve these aims, we have seen crucial legislative, political, and social initiatives endorsed, undertaken, and implemented (Grant, 2008).

It is incumbent on those who would like to see a society that defends the civil, political, and social rights of individuals, as well as one that displays empathy for and recognizes our obligations toward others, to begin to change the discourse in our nation. New discussions have to take place in local communities; in all venues of the media; in social, political, and voluntary organizations; and in face-to-face national deliberations. Fears have to be confronted, prejudices challenged, and irrational and base motives exposed as we move toward creating both a more fair and ethical nation. Franklin Roosevelt, in his second inaugural address, on January 20, 1937, observed:

> In every land there are always at work forces that drive men apart and forces that draw men together. In our personal ambitions we are individualists. But in our seeking for economic and political progress as a nation, we all go up, or else we all go down, as one people. (Roosevelt, 1937)

Thus, we also need to find and elect principled leaders committed to ideals that can advance a new social compact and move the nation onto a new path. Our recent elections have cost so much and yet informed us so little about whether the individuals running for office have the leadership abilities and moral integrity to lead the nation. We need leaders who have the capabilities to guide us through difficult decisions—decisions that may not be easy to make but are critical to our long-term future. Franklin Roosevelt recognized that a generous and compassionate nation can create security for individuals and, in turn, spur individuals to make significant contributions to the "commonwealth." In 1944, he proposed a "Second Bill of Rights" to move beyond the needed and precious civil and political rights that all citizens should have to "a new basis of security and prosperity [that] can be established for all regardless of station, need, or creed" (Roosevelt, 1944). For Roosevelt, these rights included having a "remunerative job"; "earning enough to provide adequate food, clothing, and recreation"; having a "decent home"; "having adequate medical care and the opportunity to achieve and enjoy good health"; having "adequate protection from the economic fears of old age, sickness, accident, and unemployment"; and having "a right to a good education" (Roosevelt, 1944).

Providing new deliberative opportunities, utilizing the energy of emerging social and political movements, and relying on the integrity of elected leaders may allow us to address, with both compassion and wisdom, some of the most essential issues currently facing our nation. These issues, and how we choose to respond to them, can form part of a new social compact that affirms our civil, political, and social rights and envelops those rights in an ethos that reminds us of our dependencies and impacts on each other and our obligations to future generations, other nations and their citizens, and the precious species and intricate conditions that comprise our biosphere. This is a critical moment in our history; we need to be cognizant of what kind of future we want to create together.

Notes

Chapter Seven

1 Of course, the actual ability of African Americans to vote in Southern states was not fully realized until 1965, with the passage of the Voting Rights Act (Patterson, 2000).

2 Much of the material in the following section is based on a hypothesized typology that requires further research, refinement, and verification.

3 On August 15, 2010, President Obama's job approval rating stood at 41%, compared with 69% on January 22–24, 2009. His disapproval rating on August 15, 2010, stood at 52%, compared with 13% from January 22–24, 2009. Still, President Obama's low approval ratings are not unique among modern presidents, with all "since Lyndon Johnson having suffered ratings below 40% at points in their presidencies and with several falling below 30%" (Gallup Daily, 2010; Gallup.com, 2010).

4 This would distinguish true deliberative opportunities from the raucous, uncivil, and even cruel discourse that emanated from the "town halls" designed to get input from citizens on the health care insurance legislation being considered by the Congress in the summer of 2009 (Biggs & Carey, 2009).

References

Ackerman, B., & Fishkin, J.S. (2004). *Deliberation day*. New Haven, CT: Yale University Press.

Barber, B. (1984). *Strong democracy: Participatory politics for a new age*. Berkeley: University of California Press.

Bellah, R.N. (1992). *The broken covenant: American civil religion in time of trial*. Chicago: University of Chicago Press.

Biggs, M., & Carey, N. (2009, August 7). Angry Americans disrupt town-hall healthcare talks. *Reuters*. Retrieved June 10, 2010, from http://www.reuters.com/assets/print?aid=USTRE5765QH20090807

Bohman, J., & Rehg, W. (Eds.). (1997). *Deliberative democracy: Essays on reason and politics*. Cambridge, MA: MIT Press.

Burns, J.M. (1982). *The vineyard of liberty*. New York: Vintage Books.

Cohen, J. (1997). Deliberation and democratic legitimacy. In J. Bohman & W. Rehg (Eds.), *Deliberative democracy: Essays on reason and politics* (pp. 67–91). Cambridge, MA: MIT Press.

The Constitution of the United States. (1787). *The U.S. Constitution online*. Retrieved May 20, 2010, from http://www.usconstitution.net/const.pdf

Corcoran, S.P., Romer, T., & Rosenthal, H.L. (2008). The troubled quest for equality in school finance. In H.J. Rosenthal & D.J. Rothman (Eds.), *What do we owe each other? Rights and obligations in contemporary American society* (pp. 61–77). New Brunswick, NJ: Transaction Publishers.

Dahl, R. (1985). *Controlling nuclear weapons: Democracy versus guardianship*. Syracuse, NY: Syracuse University Press.

The Declaration of Independence. (1776). *The U.S. Constitution online*. Retrieved May 20, 2010, from http://www.usconstitution.net/declar.html

De Waal, F. (2009). *The age of empathy: Nature's lessons for a kinder society*. New York: Harmony Books.

Dillon, S. (2010, August 31). Formula to grade teachers' skills gains acceptance, and critics. *The New York Times*. Retrieved September 2, 2010, from http://www.nytimes.com/2010/09/01/education/01teacher.html?src=me&ref=homepage.[

Elster, J. (1997). The market and the forum: Three varieties of political theory. In J. Bohman & W. Rehg (Eds.), *Deliberative democracy: Essays on reason and politics* (pp. 3–34). Cambridge, MA: MIT Press.

Gallup.com. (2010, August 15). *Obama sees new lows in job approval*. Retrieved August 18, 2010, from http://www.gallup.com/poll/142160/Obama-Sees-New-Lows-Job-Approval.aspx

Gallup Daily (2010, August 15). *Obama job approval*. Retrieved August 18, 2010, from http://www.gallup.com/poll/113980/Gallup-Daily-Obama-Job Approval.aspx

Giroux, H. (2010). In defense of public school teachers in a time of crisis. *Truthout.* Retrieved April 14, 2010, from http://www.truthout.org/in-defense-public-school-teachers-a-time-crisis58576?print

Grant, J.A. (2003). *Community, democracy, and the environment: Learning to share the future.* Lanham, MD: Rowman & Littlefield.

———. (2008). *The new American social compact: Rights and responsibilities in the twenty-first century.* Lanham, MD: Lexington Books.

Judt, T. (2010). *Ill fares the land.* New York: The Penguin Press.

Kline, B. (2007). *First along the river: A brief history of the U.S. environmental movement.* Lanham, MD: Rowman & Littlefield.

Leib, E.J. (2004). *Deliberative democracy in America: A proposal for a popular branch of government.* University Park: The Pennsylvania State University Press.

Mansbridge, J. (1983). *Beyond adversary democracy.* Chicago: University of Chicago Press.

Patterson, T. (2000). *We the people: A concise introduction to American politics* (3rd ed.). Boston, MA: McGraw-Hill

Pew Research Center for the People & the Press. (2010, April 1). Trust in government 1958–2010. *Distrust, discontent, anger, and partisan rancor*, Section 1. Retrieved June 4, 2010, from http://people-press.org/report/?pageid=1698

Rawls, J. (1997). The idea of public reason. In J. Bohman & W. Rehg (Eds.), *Deliberative democracy: Essays on reasons and politics* (pp. 93–144). Cambridge, MA: MIT Press.

Roosevelt, F.D. (1937, January 20). *Second inaugural address.* Retrieved September 12, 2010, from http://www.bartleby.com/124/pres50/html

———. (1944, January 11). *State of the union message to Congress.* Retrieved September 12, 2010, from http://www.presidency.ucsb.edu/ws/index.php?pid=16518

Ruffing, K., & Horney, J.R. (2010, February 17). Where today's large deficits come from: Economic downturn, financial rescues, and Bush-era policies. *Center on Budget and Policy Priorities.* Retrieved June 11, 2010, from http://www.cbpp.org/cms/index.cfm?fa=view&id=3036

Sandel, M. (1996). *Democracy's discontent: America in search of a public philosophy.* Cambridge, MA: The Belknap Press of Harvard University.

Shear, M.D., & Bacon, P., Jr. (2008, October 10). Anger is crowd's overarching emotion at McCain rally. *The Washington Post.* Retrieved June 11, 2010, from http://www.washingtonpost.com/wp-dyn/content/article/2008/10/09/AR2008100903169.html

Zernike, K., & Thee-Brenan, M. (2010, April 15). Discontent's demography: Who backs the Tea Party? *The New York Times*, p. 1.

❖ CHAPTER EIGHT ❖

Democracy's Hope

Penny S. Bryan

With the beginning of the presidential election campaign in 2008, a new movement, full of promise and hope for change, grew with the candidacy of Barack Obama. He tapped into the pulse of many in this nation with his message. In his oratory, he called us to action, to end the di/vision and begin a re/vision toward a more inclusive, just direction for the country and for the world. He led us to believe the campaign slogan and posters. Crowds at rallies shouted repeatedly, "Si se puede; Yes we can!" We would aim for the realization of our democratic principles at home and with others, respecting multiple ways of being around the world.

This hope and promise of broad-based, self-determined change "by the people" would extend to public education that could also regain some of its professional self-reliance on judgment, pluralism, and civic engagement. This hope and change would restore and strengthen our democratic society, and one of the most important ways in which to do that was through high-quality public education for all students. At the Philadelphia Constitution Center, presidential candidate Barack Obama began his remarks on race with the historic words of the Preamble to the U.S. Constitution: "We the people, in order to form a more perfect union."

Four more times in the same historic speech, Obama revisited the written Constitution and his beliefs about the assumptions on which it is based. While aspiring to the ideals and espousing its rhetoric, there is always the need to address the gaps between the ideals and the imperfect realities of every generation's time:[1]

> And yet words on a parchment would not be enough to deliver slaves from bondage or provide men and women of every color and creed their full rights and obligations as citizens of the United States. What would be needed were Americans in successive generations who were willing to do their part—through protests and struggle,

> on the streets and in the courts, through a civil war and civil disobedience and always at great risk—to narrow the gap between the promise of our ideals and the reality of their time.

In his speech, Obama explicitly committed his leadership to taking risks to narrow the gap between the ideals and imperfect realities of our democracy:

> This was one of the tasks we set forth at the beginning of this campaign—to continue the long march of those who came before us, a march for a more just, more equal, more free, more caring and more prosperous America.

He then specifically addressed the schools:

> This time we want to talk about crumbling schools that are stealing the future of black children and white children and Asian children and Hispanic children and Native American children. This time we want to reject the cynicism that tells us that these kids can't learn; that those kids who don't look like us are somebody else's problem. The children of America are not those kids, they are our kids, and we will not let them fall behind in a 21st century economy. Not this time.

He concluded his address to the current citizens:

> It is not enough to give health care to the sick or jobs to the jobless or education to our children. But it is where we start. It is where our union grows stronger. And as many generations have come to realize over the course of the two hundred and twenty one years since a band of patriots signed that document in Philadelphia, that is where the perfection begins.

Americans today still live with significant gaps between the ideal principles of democracy and the current realities of forming a more perfect union. Barack Obama expressed the position that each generation would make meaning of the lessons learned—indeed, hard earned—from the past, reconstruct them in new ways to reflect the best of what "we the people" can know and do now, and pass forward that transcendent version of ourselves so that each subsequent generation would move collectively toward a more perfect union. If we can better understand the history and current gaps between ideals and realities and the importance of the connections among principles, policies, and practices, we just might be audacious enough to bridge the chasms that confront us in public education today. The purpose of this chapter is to make the case for public educational policy that is based on democratic ideals in order to connect the dots between what we believe, say, and do.

Democracy and Education: Fragile History and Disparate Narratives

The history of democracies in the Western world is about 2,500 years old; the broken trail reveals various fragile efforts that have worked for a while, sometimes centuries, and then mostly disappeared. According to Robert Dahl (1998):

> Looking back on the rise and decline of democracy, it is clear that we cannot count on the historic forces to insure that democracy will always advance—or even survive, as the long intervals in which popular governments vanished from the earth remind us....Democracy it appears is a bit chancy. But its chances also depend on what we do ourselves. Even if we cannot count on benign historical forces to favor democracy, we are not mere victims of blind forces over which we have no control. With adequate understanding of what democracy requires and the will to meet its requirements, we can act to preserve and, what is more, to advance democratic ideas and practices. (p. 25)

From his research on democracies past and present, Dahl (1998) has concluded that in every one of them, there are gaps between the moral ideals espoused and the empirical actualities exhibited. Even given the imperfect implementations, there are certain criteria that must be present to call the governance a democracy, and none has survived longer than 400 years. The criteria are effective participation, equality in voting, gaining enlightened understanding, exercising final control over the agenda, associational autonomy for what he calls a "polyarchal" democracy, and full inclusion and participation of adults or universal suffrage. This latest criterion is almost exclusively a 20th-century phenomenon and, therefore, historically new.

America is increasingly functioning as an ahistoric nation, with little knowledge of the historic foundations of democracies and/or a related vision for democratic education. There does not seem to be widespread understanding of its fragility or the requirements for building and sustaining a society guided by its principles.

The democratic narrative for public education in America has been around since Benjamin Franklin and Thomas Jefferson (Zuckerman, 2010). Obama's idea that each generation would begin anew or continue the quest toward a more perfect union finds him standing on the shoulders of John

Dewey's philosophy for education first published nearly 100 years ago. Dewey fully developed his comprehensive explanation for the kind of education that a democratic society required in *Democracy and Education* (1916). Throughout his life, Dewey's words and works served as a midwife to progressive education, providing this new, dramatically changing nation with an alternative to the dominant culture's traditional view of education as didactic, passive, exclusively cognitive, and elitist. Dewey believed that a genuine education could only be achieved in a democratic society because of its socially and morally based reciprocal obligations to diversity, inclusion, freedom, and responsibility. William Garrison (2003) explains Dewey's ideal:

> If education is essential to democracy, we as educators also need to recognize and understand how and why the democratic values of freedom and self-governance are essential ingredients of learning and how the absence of these values in classroom practices undermines the very process of education....In failing to recognize the necessity of democracy for education, the mission of our public schools has become more focused on narrowly conceived "results." The institution of schooling is now threatening to undermine its own primary objective, that of education. (pp. 525–526)

John Dewey constructed an optimistic philosophy of education for a dynamic and diverse nation at the beginning of the 20th century, building the habits of mind and practical actions for living and learning together in order to bring about a unity across differences that would allow a society to continuously progress, to be ever adapting and building its capacity for growth.

> A democracy is more than a form of government: it is primarily a mode of associated living, of conjoint communicated experience. The extension in space of the number of individuals who participate in an interest so that each has to refer his own action to that of others, and to consider the action of others to give point and direction to his own, is equivalent of breaking down the barriers of class, race and national territory which kept men from perceiving the full import of their activity. The more numerous and more varied points of contact denote a greater diversity of stimuli to which an individual has to respond; they consequently put a premium on variation in his action. They secure a liberation of powers. (Dewey, 1916, p. 87)

We need democratic schools in order to work on renewal that will help us move in the direction of becoming a more a perfect union. Obama has the benefit of a progressive tradition for a constant reconstruction of the past to create a meaningful present and to improve the prospects for the future. He has a historic, progressive narrative to guide his redirection of public education policy. He could choose a different blueprint than the one he articulated in the fall of 2010 (Cody, 2010):

> Renewal in education, if it means anything, means creating more democratic schools in which the freedom to make choices and take action teaches each student the responsibility for his or her own learning. We need schools where teachers and students want to be—where democracy, experience and education grow and evolve, promoting a continued capacity for growth. (Garrison, 2003, p. 529)

Bourdieu (1990) echoes a similar explanation to those expressed by candidate Obama and philosopher Dewey when he suggests that societies have a choice to recapitulate the past, unchanged and fixed, or to reconstruct the past so that it continuously adapts to a changing and more equitable vision and worldview:

> We can now examine under what conditions a symbolic power can become a power of constitution, by taking the term, with Dewey, both in its philosophical sense and in its political sense: that is, a power to conserve or to transform objective principles of union and separation…the power to conserve or transform current classifications in matters of gender, nation, region, age and social status and through the words used to designate or to describe individuals, groups or institutions. To change the world, one has to change the ways of world-making, that is, the vision of the world and practical operations by which groups are produced and reproduced…symbolic efficacy depends on the degree to which the vision proposed is found in reality. (p. 137)

More recently, Paulo Freire's life's work aligned with Dewey and Bourdieu's notions of democracy. He addressed the need for a cultural revolution to redress unfair limitations in the lives of the poor and the marginalized. Consciousness and conscience are inextricably entwined in his worldview. Hence, once you know, you are compelled to act on injustice and not just individually, but institutionally and systemically. This process can lead away from limitations to freedom, from powerlessness to empowerment, and from rote routines to intelligent/intentional growth individually and the way for a society to transform itself collectively. It is a way of calling on an expanded notion of "We the people of the United States, in order to form a more perfect union…." Freire (1998) challenged us to move from what he termed the error of reproduction of the dominant ideology to—"that's just the way life is; I am powerless to change my limitations"—to transformative thinking, action, and intervention in the world. A critical, progressive pedagogy would prepare us to challenge and change the systems of limitation on marginalized groups. It would demand that people globally take risks to end the inequities in any system that limits the full knowledge and power of all the people. Obama gave us the rhetoric during his presidential campaign but not the subsequent alignment of action and educational policy.

Clearly, the question is not whether this set of ideals or Obama's concept of perfection is fully achievable by any generation. Because perfection is unachievable, some believe that we must repudiate the ideals/ideas that Obama reiterated in his speech as unrealistically utopian. They demand that we must cease to dream in the way that Freire, Mandela, King, Milk, and so many others have persuaded us is so important. Without our utopian dreams, we cannot imagine more just, sustainable realities. Langston Hughes, the 20th-century poet, reminds us that dreams are essential. They are the foundation on which hope grows and possible alternatives can be realized.

Claiming the territory of the realists, elitists reject the ideals of participatory democracy based on an inability to realize a universal and perfect implementation of them. They prefer to generate educational policy based on a version of democracy termed *guardianship* (Dahl, 1998). Guardianship democracy is governance by a small cartel of the powerful. This is what we know as a plutocracy or, in today's context, a corporatocracy. Such thinking among a group of dominant, like-minded elite is self-sealing and self-fulfilling, moving up a faulty ladder of inference (Argyris, 1990). This position of the rule of a few endures to the present and is gaining strength. It aptly describes the conscious or subconscious thinking of many. The effect of such a position is that it limits a society to perpetuate and exacerbate the inequities of the status quo and results in policies that benefit those of the elite by consolidating their disproportionate share of power over others. We see this today with a consolidation of more than 97% of this country's wealth in less than 3% of the population (Businesspundit.com, 2010; Huffington Post, 2009; Krugman, 2009; U.S. Wealth Distribution Data, 1998; Wikipedia, n.d.). There is a movement of vastly disproportionate money and political power to the top, to an elite few.

It should be argued that in a dynamic system, doing nothing is doing something. In this case, the effect of ordinary people feeling alienated, powerless, and doing nothing in a system that requires a knowledgeable and engaged citizenry may serve to weaken the democratic reality of that society. Such circular thinking and nonaction by the majority deny the constitutionally guaranteed rights of the minority population and the democratic belief in the ability of individuals and societies to grow and change peacefully through "enlightened understanding" (Dahl, 1998, p. 37) and ethical action. Democracies require freedom and self-determination. They tend to flourish in market economies with a strong middle class; however, the capitalistic economic system must be constrained from unbridled self-interest and greed by the ethical boundaries of a democratic system that requires "liberty and justice" for all. We are compelled by democracy to try to live in community with one another inclusively, peacefully, cooperatively, and fairly, both locally and globally.

The critical questions about the ability of a democracy to mature are whether these are principles worthy of aspiring to and moving toward, and what happens when we choose—consciously or unconsciously—not to heed calls to protest, struggle, and take courageous risks to dissent when we experience or witness ignorance, injustice, or hate. In other words, what happens when we are not trying or actively resisting efforts "to narrow the gap between the promise of our ideals and the reality of [our] time" (Obama, 2008)? Isn't turning over the determination and direction of a society to a few "doing something" that quite profoundly perpetuates or even strengthen the gaps? Isn't this true whether it is Wall Street, Main Street, or public education? Like Sisyphus, we need to keep pushing the boulder up the mountain, even though we know we will not reach the top (even by "racing" there, as Arne Duncan advocates). However, at least we will be moving in the direction of equity and democratic principles.

Dewey contended that a democratic society only thrives and sustains itself through universal education that is aligned with that society's basic purposes and principles. We can ask ourselves to what degree is full inclusion of the numerous and varied interests of all the citizens and how open is the free flow of all the information, and the interaction and movement of all the people.

> The devotion of democracy to education is a similar fact. The superficial explanation is that a government resting upon popular suffrage cannot be successful unless those, who elect and who obey their governors, are educated. Since a democratic society repudiates the principle of external authority, it must find a substitute in voluntary disposition and interest; these can be created only by education. But there is a deeper explanation. *A democracy is more than a form of government; it is primarily a mode of associated living, of conjoint communicated experience.* (Dewey, 1916; italics in original)

Democracy and Public Education: Guardianship Model

Where does public education seem to be headed in this administration? Is it heading toward strengthening the concepts and responsibilities of democratic beliefs and political culture or weakening and diminishing this capacity? Is anyone serious about connecting democratic principles to public educational policy in the United States? This administration presented itself to the American people during the campaign as based on "Respect, empower and include" (Mendez, 2009, p. 13). How then is it dealing in public education with the current reality of strong subcultural diversity, a condition that threatens to weaken a democratic society if not handled well? Where is the accountability to the public in fulfilling the needs of public education in a democracy for pluralism, civic engagement, dissent, and democratic deliberation across strong subcultural differences? It was included in the rhetoric of candidate Obama's landmark address on race in Philadelphia. Where can we find this kind of accountability in the Race to the Top ($4.3 billion) that included the anticipated overhaul of No Child Left Behind or the Investing in Innovation Fund ($675 million) and stimulus law for school reform ($3 billion approved by Congress in 2009)?

The resources for public education are inadequate, and programs mandated remain underfunded. The largest one time federal spending on public education, the federal stimulus program monies, $100 billion, will be almost completely gone by the end of 2010. Strong middle-class jobs and economic markets do affect the financial health of public school funding. Districts and states, already devastated by the economic recession, are approaching what is called "a funding cliff" in terms of public education.

> The monies were allocated as follows: $39.5 billion as part of a stabilization fund intended to bolster the finances of state public education systems, $13 billion for poor students, Title I, and $12.2 billion for students with disabilities. Congress directed the rest of the $100 billion to smaller initiatives including $4.3 billion to a school improvement grant program and what the Obama administration calls Race to the Top. (Dillon, 2010)

Together, Secretary of Education Duncan and President Obama have issued a Race to the Top plan for funding public education reform; we have already examined the flawed concept of perfection and/or the notion of reaching such a place. In addition to an unachievable "top," we would do well to ask: Race to the top of what and for what purpose? David Brooks

(2009) refers to Rahm Emanuel calling it the "Quiet Revolution." Quietly, $4.3 billion of our tax money has been put in a pot with a small opening, fostering an economic model not constrained by the social and moral principles of liberty and justice for all. It is a public/private funding distribution based on a competitive model for states with a few winners making it to the top and all the remainder losers, which means that most of our students lose as well. It promotes funding with a standardized delivery that necessitates conformity to a one-size-fits-all definition of learning, entrance by lotteries, and success defined as high test scores. The vast majority of those who don't or won't fit all the requirements are the losers. Whatever happened to the democratic notion of a publicly funded, universal right to a free, high-quality education with pluralistic views and many ways of knowing for all our children? What an irony considering the major education policy in place since 2001 is called No Child Left Behind.

In Arne Duncan's policy platform for K–12 public education, there seems to be no substantive change or revision from the previous administration. There seems to be more image perception than substance in doing anything differently (Cunningham, 2010). From the point of view of our democratic principles, there is not the reality of "starting here," as Obama's speech encouraged us to believe, to change direction. Instead it is still the elite guardianship view of power, politics, and public education that prevails, promulgated by the previous administration of President George W. Bush and Secretary of Education Margaret Spellings.

Understanding such a model helps to explain what appear to be some strange but strategic connects and disconnects. For example, there is an ongoing, unsubstantiated insistence on connecting student performance and teacher pay. In Arne Duncan's words (as cited in Klein, 2009): "Teacher evaluation in this country is fundamentally broken….In a country where teacher evaluation is largely divorced from student progress, student success, how do you defend that?" He reiterated that the administration still places a major value on merit pay, saying that the federal Teacher Incentive Fund, which gives grants to school districts for performance pay programs, was the best thing the previous administration did (Klein, 2009).

How are teachers valued in this guardian class, factory model? Giroux (2009) contends that Obama and Duncan want to treat teachers as low-skilled factory workers by creating market-based notions of reward and competitiveness, all based on a series of values that have been utterly discredited for causing the financial meltdown the country now faces. This market-based ideology being resurrected by Obama and Duncan has not only altered economic agendas throughout the world but has also transformed politics, restructured social relations, and produced an array of reality narratives and disciplinary measures that normalize its perverted view of citizenship, the state, and the supremacy of market relations (Giroux, 2009).

There seems to be deliberate resistance to listening to competent, highly qualified, experienced teachers—those closest to implementation. If the country sincerely wants no child to be left behind, then it does not seem to make sense to pay teachers based on high test scores, because it is precisely the most fragile learners who are also often the poor and subsequently poor test takers. They are the ones who have the most need for teachers' expertise and efforts in order not to be left behind. These students need more time on experiential and holistic sense making and less time on rote learning through work sheets, test prep, and mind-numbing test taking. Students who are marginalized in the system are not starting the "race" on an even playing field, and no one races with mastery on their first try. They stumble, practice, and, with encouragement, persistence, and new knowledge, begin to improve. They don't improve when they are judged by one narrow measure of learning and then bombarded with negative messages of blame, humiliation, and failure. No one does!

Why would someone choose to teach children with special needs—children who are just learning to speak English, and children who have not had a wide variety of dominant-culture educational opportunities, resources, and experiences? Why would a teacher want to be placed in a school community where there is a high turnover; a heightened struggle for adequate food (hungry is now called "food insecure"); stable, safe shelter; access to competent health care; and adequate employment? Doesn't this system seem to place its highest value and rewards on teaching a population of the dominant culture and the children of the guardian class whose higher socioeconomic levels, research has determined, give them the best chance of scoring well on high-stakes, standardized tests?

By successfully tying these two features together in educational policy, teachers get the blame exclusively (except for the portion blamed on the students) when students do not succeed on narrow, flawed measures of success—the standardized tests. In Chicago, Duncan closed scores of schools and transferred all the children. Follow-up research indicates that those who went to similar schools continued to do poorly on tests and those who went to schools with higher-performing test takers improved their test scores (Dillon, 2010). This narrowed, flawed reasoning sets up a cycle of blame, punishment, failure, and school closings, and dissolution-disillusion that research has not shown to have made a positive difference in Chicago, where Duncan tried it.

The situation was examined in the unflattering film *Waiting for Superman* (2010). Oprah Winfrey's television show (September 2010) promoted the film. Oprah's guests were Davis Guggenheim, the movie director; Bill Gates, the corporate philanthropist; and Michelle Rhee, then Chancellor of the Washington, DC, schools; as well as a select few charter school leaders, who each received $1 million for their schools on the air. The representative group illustrates how powerfully the guardian forces of wealth can impact and shape public education. Even if highly well intentioned, those with media, administrative, and corporate wealth and power are the ones influencing public policy. We must ask: Whose voices are not heard? Where is the space and legitimization for those who believe that high-stakes standardized test scores are a flawed and unfair way to assess teaching and that overreliance on this one indicator narrows and fragments the curriculum, impoverishes what is considered learning, and structurally/emotionally results in lethal stress fractures of a public institution perhaps most responsible for what this society will be like in the future?

Recently, this same cycle of blame has extended beyond the K–12 practitioners to those who prepare them—the postsecondary professors of education at colleges and universities. Placing blame on the academy seems to resonate with the corporate elite with whom Arne Duncan seems to be most closely aligned. There is a lot of rhetoric about "highly qualified teachers" and professional development funds, again pushed more as deficits to be remediated than as respect for educators and support for professional growth, with special appreciation of those willing to try to meet the exponentially increasing demands of educating a diverse population in a stiflingly narrow curriculum. President Ronald Reagan used this thinking in the 1980s when he said that big government was the problem and not the solution, while continuing to grow the size of government on his watch. It is a stance that assigns unilateral blame while ignoring the complexity of contributing social factors, gains political capital, and demoralizes and stigmatizes those on whom the blame is heaped. All of this negativity persists under No Child Left Behind despite the lack of credible educational research to back it up.

Another way to assess current realities for democratic schooling is to examine the blurring of civic, military, and private institutions participating in and/or helping to fund public education. These military, civic, and public/private partnerships, some extremely effective and well meaning like the Gates Foundation, and others more self-serving, still dilute the power of the public and ordinary people. There is disproportionate power coming from wealthy, private, corporate, and military voices. The result is the semi-privatization and semi-militarization of one of our greatest democratic institutions—the public school. There is also a clash of primary purpose and the diluting of accountability by the public institution to the public for high-quality education and human rights for all the nation's children. The unintended consequence may be a widening of the economic, cultural, and educational gaps in a society that aspires to sustain its democracy in times of scarce resources and growing acrimony regarding differences.

Arne Duncan's success as superintendent of the Chicago School District was the initiation of five military academies in the most fragile neighborhoods of inner-city Chicago. A culture of militarization relies on hierarchy, externally mandated controls, and extrinsic rewards. It is guided by unquestioning obedience to authority of a few over most of the population, with the children and their families at the bottom of the power grid. The teachers are a combination of military and civilians. The dominant educational philosophy is that the teacher is exclusively the one with the knowledge of the one right answer. It is replete with top-down leadership and the example of military careers more highly visible than other choices at a time when the country is fighting two wars and needs recruits. Such a system appears to the undiscriminating public as though order is being imposed on chaos, and that somehow this law and order equates to education. I would ask: Where are the values of critical and creative thinking in these schools? Where are the voices of pluralism, dissent, and creative expression developed?

The prevailing educational philosophy views traditional government as the "strict father" (Lakoff, 2004). In education, this means that those at the top have used their power to paternalistically name the single indicator of academic success and to marginalize and even criminalize those who, in their view, have failed. Governmental political bureaucrats assume the role of "decider"; they assign blame and then punish those who don't measure up to a single standardization for what they define as excellence in an increasingly aggressive and egregious manner. This misguided and damaging governance persists, however ill conceived or unattainable the standards and measurements are. When a school or district reaches an advanced level of failure under such a deficit-based system as the one now in place, it is totally disbanded and reconfigured in the narrow image of what the guardian class constitutes as success. Instead of working with many public educators and their constituent organizations, there has been a tendency to blame them as insiders who are responsible for the problems. There has been a marginalization of dissenting voices from groups such as unions, professional organizations, and progressive academia. The inside voices have been discredited and seen as adversaries. Tellingly, 20% of our teaching force leaves the profession in the first 5 years (Tye & Obrien, 2002). I fear that it might be the best 20% who cannot endure the lack of autonomy in exercising their judgment and professional craft.

In an era of terrorism, war, gangs, hate crimes, and domestic violence, there is an increasing permeation of violence throughout society and concomitant fears of violence (Education Update, 2009). This begets a culture based on fear, whereas the fragile essence and contribution of a democracy are based on the hope of sustaining peaceful and deliberate social change. The public, including the children, is constantly subjected to a barrage of sensationalist media communication that glorifies hate speech and physical violence. It appears in media talk shows, video games, the Internet, and movies. The administration's policies, such as that of "Zero Tolerance," seem to go against its own rhetoric. Its actions result in blaming, demonizing, and criminalizing the poor and others who are different.

The Zero Tolerance policy is an example of this kind of thinking in public schools. Children as young as age 6 have been taken out of school, in front of their peers, in adult-sized handcuffs by the police to the police station and booked (Herbert, 2010). Their crimes were things like an escalating temper tantrum, bringing a camping knife to school to cut an apple, or having a Tylenol. This is another example of a policy that falsely reasons that by treating everyone the same, you are treating everyone fairly. It is predicated on a one-size-fits-all schema, and it results in the most unjust treatment and dehumanization of children, who are most vulnerable. For those children punished in this way and those who witness it, the lessons learned are not about fairness, justice, and democracy.

There is another dehumanizing connection made by this administration between global education and technology. It is focusing on increasing the technological tools and knowledge needed by all citizens in the 21st century. This emphasis is not controversial, and closing the digital divide can be a positive move toward equity, but a danger lurks here as well. The danger is in assuming that human understanding and empathy can come about while students never leave the screen, virtually traversing the world in an isolated cubicle in front of a machine.

If there is to be deep understanding and empathy across vast subcultural differences and through new literacies that are changing our cultural learning environment, there is still the need to meet and touch, not only virtually or in affinity groups, but in person and place, and to learn how to live conjointly in proximal and virtual community with others over time.

Bullying may be the most common type of violence in schools today. It is reported that almost 30% of U.S. teens are either bullies or the targets of bullying, or both. Most bullying incidents last less than a minute, with cyber-bullying via instant messaging or mass e-mails (or video streaming) occurring almost instantaneously. Bullying is defined as a pattern of intentional harm done over time that takes physical, verbal, or proxemic forms. The last form translates into exclusion through social or personal distance, thus harming relationships (Amstutz & Mullet, 2005).

The rise of cyberbullying (Hoffman, 2010) and related teen suicides (Curwen, 2010) further emphasize the need for the moral constraints that democratic principles provide. The purpose of public education goes deeper than mere access to knowledge and tools; it must connect to those democratic values of respect and human dignity—full inclusion and universal suffrage, and the need to find common goals and interests with which to shape a society that works for the common good.

There seem to be some dangerous realities in a corporate-driven culture that dominates educational policy and that has as its primary purpose and goal the production of a highly technical, deferentially obedient, economic workforce. No Child Left Behind and the educational reforms of the previous and current administrations appear to be flawed policies that weaken perhaps our greatest public institution—public schooling. They are so narrowly focused and dangerously fragmented that the effect is to dilute both democracy and public education. Current policies reduce pedagogy to a didactic, technical, and technological system of domesticated rote training.

> [W]e are moving students farther away from those skills that "expert citizens" need to lead productive lives: creativity, common sense, wisdom, ethics, dedication, honesty, teamwork, hard work, how to win and lose, fair play, lifelong learning. (Sternberg, 2007–2008; cited in Gallagher, 2009, p. 116)

Semi-privatization through public–private partnerships, even while doing some positive good, and school choice/charters still open themselves to operating at cross purposes to our democratic principles. The boundaries between the common good and private gain are blurred, because they eliminate clear separations between what is public and what is private. Learning and funding are competitive; most lose while a few win it all. Privately funded public structures in institutions can siphon energy and weaken a single education system accessible and accountable to its public for educating all children. Our public libraries seem to be following the same path as public schools. "In Santa Clarita, California, a private company from Maryland has taken over public libraries…growing into the country's fifth largest library system….I can't think of anything that's been lost," says a citizen and volunteer from Redding, California (Streetfield, 2010). This private, for-profit company does the hiring and buys the books.

The Obama administration's chasm between rhetoric and reality is not the only expressed example of such a dilemma or paradox between our principles and our actions in public education. That is, although schools are charged with promoting a discourse of democracy, they often put structures in place that undermine the substantive democratic principles they claim to teach. As a result, schools are necessarily engaged in a pedagogy of lies that are shaped and supported by the interplay of the media, business interests, and the academic enterprise (Macedo; cited in Zinn, 1995).

Democracy's Hope for a New Vision and Reality

What are the alternative possibilities and responsibilities for those who believe that a politics of fear with an overemphasis on high-stakes standardized testing in select areas of the curriculum, top-down punishment, shaming of children, destruction of existing school communities, and narrow economic and educational models of educational reform are not working (Cody, 2010)? They weaken not only public education but our democracy as well. A genuine, democratic education is the vehicle capable of narrowing the gaps between the ideal and the real, the moral and the social in society.

Schools and educational policy deliberations need to be reorganized for democratic discourse and democratic goals, not bureaucratic, media, business, or political expediency. As so many educators have stated, a democracy requires opportunities and experiences to develop the whole child (Eisner, 2005; Kohn, 2005; Noddings, 2005) with open, serious habits of mind and heart, to know the purpose as well as the content of what they are studying, to learn for real reasons in many forms, and to make meaningful connections so that they can bring and adapt that learning to new situations. Only when they are the subjects of their own intentional learning and know themselves as well can they anticipate, contemplate, and dream about a future with possibilities and alternatives to the present. Only then can it be called education and not mere rote training. It is with an education of the whole child, who enters the classroom feeling safe, welcomed unconditionally, and confident about him or herself and his or her capacity to learn, that the critical and creative thinking and acting required to sustain a democratic society can occur.

It is only when there is a seamless integration of meaning and real life, connections in and out of school, that authentic and enduring education can take place. New literacies have lent urgency to the necessity of redefining what we mean by learning spaces. Some are now calling them opportunity spaces, and they occur in lots of diverse places, often linked by several sites and learning modalities. Thus, significant learning cannot be measured by a one-size-fits-all, narrowly defined time, place, and factoid. However financed, by public funds or private resources of the rich, the essential criterion is the adherence to democratic principles. When politics and policies that are vastly different from No Child Left Behind support intellectual and humane architecture and civic engagement, then such a society can hope and act for a better future.

Numerous organizations are trying to democratize public schools and keep the system fair and strong. Their ideals and their actions align. Some who are working in this way are The Forum for Education and Democracy and its partner Rethink Learning Now, The Five Freedoms Network, the First Amendment Schools, Coalition of Essential Schools, Fairtest, ASCD's Education of the Whole Child, and the Dignity in Schools Campaign National Resolution for Ending School Pushout. The last effort is supported by 180 organizations from across the country, including the International Institute for Restorative Practices:

> [A] call to action for our school systems to end hard discipline polices and law enforcement tactics that push too many young people out of school each year. The resolution calls for schools to implement positive alternatives that protect the human rights of young people and keep students in school, including "evidence based" discipline policies and practices. ("Dignity in Schools," 2009)

Restorative Discipline in schools is one such effort. Restorative Justice, the larger movement and the basis for the Restorative Discipline programs in schools, has been adopted by the Oakland California Unified School District and by a number of schools in Berkeley, California, as the official policy for handling discipline (D. Yusem, private conversations with author, May–June 2010). The program and the philosophy of Restorative Discipline in schools and communities are based on an inclusive look at who has been harmed and creative possibilities for healing and moving toward wholeness and health rather than punishment and alienation. Practices aim to change individuals and communities by dealing with the harm done to all affected, meeting all the needs with care, so that they can heal and become healthy. It is discipline that restores individuals and communities that have been harmed or damaged.

We have to deliberately set out to build our schools as caring communities and democratic institutions so that our students—as children and, later, adults—can practice universally safe, responsible, engaged citizenship in a democratic model of education. We can help public schools foster citizenship and connect the dots between living, learning, and leading together.

> The idea that teachers take responsibility for their collective, not just individual, work carries over to other workplaces and communities….The importance of face to face encounters between people with differing views and the related capacity to imagine a viewpoint different from one's own are intellectual habits of mind, central to our academic work, our school governance and the governance of the larger society….At every point in our work, we must connect the dots between our practice and democracy….What price are we willing to pay for putting democracy at the head of the line? Whatever answer to that question we come up with, the price of not asking it at all…is immeasurably higher. (Meier, 2003, p. 20)

Obama's (2008) rhetoric in Philadelphia had the promise of working for a more perfect union through one of this country's greatest institutions public education. But that rhetoric has not matched his administration's actions. We need new words, and we definitely need to connect to new actions.

Giroux (2009) explains that this administration's "view of education is stuck in reverse":

> We do need some new language to define the meaning and purpose of public and higher education, one that makes democracy its defining principle of both learning and everyday classroom practices....This is a view of education that treats teachers as critical and supportive intellectuals, students as engaged citizens, not consumers, and schools as democratic public spheres, not training sites for the business world. It is also a view of education in which matters of power, equality, civic literacy and justice are central to any viable notion of education that addresses the future in terms of its democratic possibilities, rather than the bottom line. (Giroux, 2009)

We do have choices—not always for what happens to us, such as the deep economic, global recession, but in how we choose to respond. We can either be our best selves as an empathic, just collective, or we can reflect our lesser selves and react narrowly to calculated self-interest and greed. We can move further in the direction of a rule of the guardian class, or we can reshape ourselves more equitably. In this chapter, I have tried to lay out the evidence and arguments for democratically driven educational policy based on both our past history and greatest possibilities for the future.

We need our dreams. Hope is a choice. Do we have the audacity? Howard Zinn (1995), in the final paragraphs of *You Can't Be Neutral on a Moving Train*, tells us:

> To be hopeful in bad times is not just foolishly romantic. It is based on the fact that human history is a history not only of cruelty, but also of compassion, sacrifice, courage, and kindness....What we choose to emphasize in this complex history will determine our lives. If we see only the worst, it destroys our capacity to do something. If we remember those times and places and there are so many—where people have behaved magnificently, this gives us the energy to act, and at least the possibility of sending this spinning top of a world in a different direction. (p. 209)

Closing this democratic gap among our ideals, possible dreams, and current realities is the most important work at every level of education in a democracy. It has been so for more than 200 years. Educators and politicians are the public intellectuals, professionals accountable to the public trust and its citizens for designing and realizing a quality education for all children in alignment with democratic principles. We must change direction now and expand our languages, policies, and practices to construct a richer landscape for imagination, thinking, and learning in democratic deliberation and in community with each other. I urge the current administration to relisten and commit to President Obama's words in Philadelphia, to review the promises made during the campaign, and to make those our realities for public education. To paraphrase Zinn, there is no such thing as being neutral on a moving train. In a mature democracy, the burden and beauty is that only "we the people" can decide, push, prod, and demand that our government move us toward policies that actualize our ideals and dreams.

In writing about mid-20th-century public school desegregation in Little Rock's Central High School, Supreme Court Justice Stephen Breyer (2010) recounts a move toward closing one of the historic gaps between our ideals and realities:

> Today only a mile away from Central High, one can find the grave of the wife of the Cherokee Chief Ross. That grave marks the spot where she died on the Trail of Tears on her way to Oklahoma—after the government evicted her and her fellow Cherokees from the Georgian lands. The grave and the school together tell a story about acceptance and the rule of law in America. Although the distance between the grave and the school is small, the nation had come a long way in the time in between the two decisions that they symbolize. It was moving in the right direction. (pp. 66–67)

"We the people" means all of us, and we can *begin here* to take responsibility to draft a different kind of public education vision-policy-reality. Yes, we can move toward closing the gaps for "*a more perfect union.*" Democracy's best hope depends on the historic understanding and current will of the people to insist on a strong system of universal public education as a human right; the best way to ensure an enduring public identity with liberty and justice for all is to hold fast to our dreams and bind them steadfastly to democratic principles and actions.

> With liberty and justice for all—
> But for whom?
> Like the winter's frost kissing summer's sweet garden
> The mind's eye catches glimpses—sound bites of another side.
> —Jennifer Allen

Note

Chapter Eight

1 Quotations immediately following refer to Obama's 2008 speech.

References

Allen, J. (2004, May 20). Into the light. Excerpted and adapted from an unpublished poem, Graduate Student Creative Expression Assignment for Education 655, Education, Democracy and Social Change, Chapman University, College of Educational Studies.

Amstutz, L.S., & Mullet, J.H. (2005). *The little book of restorative discipline in schools* (The Little Books of Justice and Peacebuilding Series). Intercourse, PA: Good Books.

Argyris, C. (1990). *Overcoming organizational defenses*. Boston: Allyn & Bacon.

Bourdieu, P. (1990). *In other words: Essays towards a reflexive sociology*. Palo Alto, CA: Stanford University Press.

Breyer, S. (2010). *Making our democracy work*. New York: Alfred A. Knopf.

Brooks, D. (2009, October 23). Opinion: The quiet revolution. *The New York Times*. Available at www.newyorktimes.org

Businesspundit.com. (2010, February 8). *Wealth distribution in the United States*. Available at www.Businesspundit.com

Cody. A. (2010, September 17). *Education reform has jumped the shark*. Retrieved October 10, 2010, from blogs.edweek.org/teachings/living-in-dialogue/

Cunningham, C. (2010, January 21). *Education policy blog*. Available at www.blogspot.com

Curwen, T. (2010, October 8). Gay teen endured a daily gauntlet. *Los Angeles Times*. Available at www.latimes.com/news/local/la-me-sethwalsh

Dahl, R. (1998). *On democracy*, New Haven, CT: Yale University Press.

Dewey, J. (1916). *Democracy and education: An introduction to the philosophy of education*. New York: Macmillan.

Dignity in Schools Campaign releasing national resolution for ending school pushout. (2009). *Restorative practices*. Retrieved December 13, 2010, from www.eforum 2009

Dillon, S. (2010, February 7). Education: With federal stimulus money gone, schools face budget gaps. *The New York Times*. Available at www.newyorktimes.org

Education. (n.d.). With federal stimulus money gone, many schools face budget gaps. *The New York Times*. Available at www.newyortktimes.org

Education Update. (2009, December). *Keeping schools safe from gangs*. Alexandria, VA: Association for Supervision and Curriculum Development.

———. (2010, February). *Race to the top program rolls out*. Alexandria, VA: Association for Supervision and Curriculum Development.

Eisner, E. (2005, September). *Back to whole: Educational leadership*. Alexandria, VA: Association for Supervision and Curriculum Development.

Freire, P. (1998). *Pedagogy of freedom: Ethics, democracy and civic courage*. London: Rowman & Littlefield.

Gallagher, K. (2009). *Readicide*. Portland, ME: Stenhouse Publishers.

Garrison, W.H. (2003, March). Democracy, experience, and education: Promoting a continued capacity for growth. *Phi Delta Kappan, 84*(7), 525–529.

Giroux, H. (2009, July 24). Retrieved February 7, 2010, from truthout.org

Guggenheim, D. (2010). *Waiting for Superman* [Documentary film].

Herbert, B. (2007, April 9). 6-year-olds under arrest. *The New York Times*, p. 1.

Herbert, B. (2010, March 6). Opinion: Cops vs. kids. *The New York Times*, p. A19.

Hoffman, J. (2010, June 27). Online bullies pull schools into the fray. *The New York Times.* Retrieved June 28, 2010, from www.newyorktimes.com

Holladay, J. (2010, Fall). *Cyberbullying: The stakes have never been higher for students or schools: Teaching tolerance.* Montgomery, AL: Southern Poverty Law Center.

Huffington Post. (2009, September 14). *Income inequality is at an all-time high: Study.* Retrieved February 8, 2010, from www.Huffingtonpost.com

Hughes, L. (2010, July 9). Dreams. Available at www.poemhunter.com

Karp, S. (2010, Spring). School reform we can't believe in. *Rethinking Schools, 24*(3), 48–53.

Klein, A. (2009, November 30). *Education Week.* Available at www.edweek.org

Kohn, A. (2005, September). *Unconditional teaching, educational leadership.* Alexandria, VA: Association for Supervision and Curriculum Development.

Krugman, P. (2009, August 13). *Even more gilded. The conscience of a liberal.* Available at www.krugman.blogs.nytimes.com

Lakoff, G. (2004). *Don't think of an elephant: Know your values and frame the debate.* White River Junction, VT: Chelsea Green Publishing.

Meier, D. (2003, September). What does it take to build a school for democracy? *Phi Delta Kappan, 85*(1), 15–21.

Mendez, B.E. (November 23, 2009). The Obama Generation Revisited, *The Nation. 289*(17), 13.

Noddings, N. (2005, September). *What does it mean to educate the whole child? Educational Leadership.* Alexandria, VA: Association for Supervision and Curriculum Development.

Obama, B. (2008, March 18). Transcript of campaign speech on race, Philadelphia Constitution Center. Available at www.newyortktimes.com

Streetfield, D. (2010, September 27). Outsourcing fairly healthy libraries and hearing a roar. *The New York Times*, pp. 1, 11.

Tye, B.B., & Obrien, L. (2002). Why are experienced teachers leaving the profession? *Phi Delta Kappan, 84*(1), 24–32.

U.S. wealth distribution data. (1998). Retrieved February 8, 2010, from www.L-Curve.org

Wikipedia. (n.d.). *Wealth in the United States.* Retrieved February 8, 2010, from www.En.wikipedia.org/wiki/Wealth_in_the_United_States

Zinn, H. (1995). *You can't be neutral on a moving train.* Boston: Beacon Press.

Zinn, H., & Macedo, D. (2005). *On democratic education* (Series in Critical Narrative). Boulder, CO: Paradigm Publishers.

Zuckerman, M. (2010, September/October). Paternity test. *The Pennsylvania Gazette*, *109*(1), 41–45.

Afterword

Stella C. Batagiannis

The authors of the chapters in this book and the citizens of this nation have analyzed and agonized over the stated philosophy of President Barack Obama, his political actions, and the seeming contradictions between the two. *The Hope for Audacity: From Cynicism to Hope in Educational Leadership and Policy* is an expression of our voices, a reminder of the fragility of our nation's democracy, a challenge to President Obama to be authentic, and a plea to allow us to work with him to effect educational change that can work—meaningful reform.

These authors remind President Obama that democracy and education are inextricably linked. Thus, education must remain a public good, a means of building community, not be diminished to a mere market. It is our belief in President Obama's capacity to see beyond the murky politics of market logic and to feel compassion for those without power and political voice that has fueled our hope. Although we, as educators, have the responsibility to honestly critique current educational policy because we experience its deleterious effects daily, we do not aspire to critique mired in cynicism, but in stubborn hope. We agree with the words of Barry Kanpol (Chapter 1 in this volume): "It is easy to critique as a way out of dealing with authentic change efforts" (p. 4). While expressing strong concern for the educational decisions that the President has made, Kanpol also challenges educators to rise beyond cynicism and move to creative action.

Because President Obama's election symbolized hope—for authentic education and a renewal of democracy—giving up on him is also admitting that the light of possibility is gone. So, while we analyze and point out values and dispositions that Obama has not reflected or actions that contradict his stated beliefs, our hope remains that he will listen to our voices, remember his own words, and modify his policies and actions accordingly. We dare still to hope that President Obama's own professed philosophy of hope will inform his political action and that he will have the audacity to act with courage and strength. We continue to hope he will remember that we stand ready to support him and help him lead in education, which, ultimately, will be the light of this nation and our democracy—or not.

About the Authors

STELLA C. BATAGIANNIS is Associate Professor of Educational Leadership in the College of Education and Public Policy at Indiana University-Purdue University Fort Wayne. Previously, she served for more than 30 years in K–12 education in Indiana as a superintendent, principal, and teacher. Much of her leadership work has been in urban districts. She earned her PhD in Educational Administration from Indiana State University. Her research interests are in qualitative research focused on courage in leadership, the dispositions of leadership, the Scholarship of Teaching and Learning (SoTL), and action research. Her publications include: "The Quest for Instantaneous Perfection and the Demand for 'Push-Button' Administration," *The Educational Forum* (2009); "Leadership Guided by Courage: A Challenge to Instantaneous Perfection," *Journal of Educational Thought* (2007); "A Lesson in Courage," in K. Arnoff (Ed.), *So to Teach* (2007); and "Promise and Possibility for Aspiring Principals: An Emerging Leadership Identity through Learning to Do Action Research," *The Qualitative Report* (2011). She serves as co-editor of *scholarlypartnershipsedu.*

PENNY S. BRYAN is Associate Professor in the College of Educational Studies at Chapman University. She earned her PhD at the University of Pennsylvania. Her areas of professional interest are leadership, literacy, democracy, and the importance of the relationships of the creative process in education and society. She advocates for legitimizing the roles of arts and restorative practices in education for a healthy, just society. She has authored, presented, chaired, and conducted workshops at the American Educational Research Association, the Association of Moral Education, and the International Reading Association, as well as numerous local, state, national, and international conferences. She has also written and presented with colleagues, graduate students, their students, and K–12 educators. She has served as Senior Editor, Editor, and Associate Editor of the statewide academic journal *The Journal of Educational Leadership and Administration: Teaching and Program Development*.

BRIAN L. FIFE is Professor of Public Policy in the College of Education and Public Policy at Indiana University-Purdue University Fort Wayne. His published works include *Desegregation in American Schools: Comparative Intervention Strategies*; *School Desegregation in the Twenty-First Century: The Focus Must Change*; *Higher Education in Transition: The Challenges of the New Millennium*; *Political Culture and Voting Systems in the United States: An Examination of the 2000 Presidential Election*; and *Reforming the Electoral Process in America: Toward More Democracy in the 21st Century*. He is currently working on a book on public education and the common school ideal in the United States. His background is in political science, and he has a PhD and an MA from the State University of New York at Binghamton and a BA from the University of Maine.

JANE A. GRANT is Professor and Chair of the Department of Public Policy at Indiana University-Purdue University Fort Wayne. She received her PhD in Sociology from the University of California, Berkeley. Her publications include *The New American Social Compact: Rights and Responsibilities in the Twenty-First Century* (Lexington Books, 2008) and *Community, Democracy, and the Environment: Learning to Share the Future* (Rowman & Littlefield, 2003). Her current research continues to examine the development of a new American social compact.

JONATHAN C. HILPERT is Assistant Professor in the College of Education and Public Policy at Indiana University-Purdue University Fort Wayne. He is a former high school teacher. He received his PhD in Educational Psychology from Arizona State University in 2008. His recent publications focus on the role of motivation, cognition, and personal beliefs in learning about scientific information. He has received funding from the National Science Foundation for his work in young adult learning about science, specifically focused on student engagement in post-secondary engineering classrooms. His current research focuses on the application and specification of domain general learning models to STEM and health-related learning contexts.

BARRY KANPOL is Dean of the College of Education and Public Policy at Indiana University-Purdue University Fort Wayne. His research, which includes 12 books and more than 75 articles, has linked the "critical" role of teachers in the social order to race, class, and gender structural configurations. He has published in such journals as *Harvard Educational Review*, *Educational Theory*, *Journal of Educational Thought*, *Educational Foundations*, and *Urban Review*, among many others. Some of his most popular books include *Critical Pedagogy: An Introduction*; *Issues and Trends in Critical Pedagogy*; *Teachers Talking Back and Breaking Bread*; *Critical Multiculturalism: Uncommon Voices in a Common Struggle*; *From Nihilism to Possibility: Democratic Transformations for the Inner City and Teacher Education*; and *Urban Education: The Move from the Traditional to the Pragmatic*. As dean, his current research agenda involves a deeper understanding of how Colleges of Education and universities go about building a "public identity," one that concurrently challenges a neoliberal social agenda while building liberating college structures that link curriculum and research to impactful community engagement. He received his PhD from The Ohio State University. He is married with four children.

KATHLEEN A. MURPHEY is Professor of Education and Associate Dean in the College of Education and Public Policy at Indiana University-Purdue University Fort Wayne. She researches educational history, policy, and reform. Currently she is studying desegregation in Fort Wayne and the surrounding county and has previously researched the history of the educational workforce in Fort Wayne during the 19th century: "In the Shadow of *Brown*," *scholarlypartnershipsedu* (2007); "Common School or One Best System? Tracking School Reform in Fort Wayne, Indiana, 1853 1875," *Historical Studies in Education/Revue d'histoire de l'education* (1999). She has also written about the history and impact of teacher unions and the impact of educational reform on teacher educators work: "NCATE and the Restructuring of Teacher Educators Work: A Labor Process Perspective," in Swim et al., *Teacher National Accreditation as Community Dialogue: Transformative Reflections* (2010). She completed her doctoral work at the Harvard Graduate School of Education.

MARISOL REXACH is Curriculum Specialist in Santa Ana, California. She holds a BA in Education and an MA in Curriculum and Instruction. She is currently pursuing a PhD in Cultural and Curricular Studies at Chapman

University. She is the pro bono Educational Director for a small, nonprofit Saturday school for Sudanese children who reside in Southern California. Her research interests relate to cultural discontinuity between home and school and transformational education, with particular emphasis on global and integrated education and the partnership model.

KENNETH TYE is Professor Emeritus in Education at Chapman University. Before retiring from Chapman, he taught graduate comparative education and curriculum classes, was Chair of the Education Department, and was Assistant Provost for International Programs for the university. Since his retirement, he has done part-time teaching and other tasks for the College of Educational Studies. Ken spent 14 years as Program Officer for a research center affiliated with UCLA. Earlier, he was a social studies teacher and school principal. Ken earned his BA degree from San Francisco State, his MA degree from San Diego State, and his EdD from UCLA with a cognate in political science. He attended Yale for a National Defense Education Act Institute in African History and Ethnology. He has worked in several countries in Africa, Asia, Europe, and the Middle East, as well as Australia and New Zealand. Ken has more than 70 publications to his credit, including five books.

TOM WILSON is a faculty member and Director of the Paulo Freire Democratic Project in the College of Educational Studies at Chapman University. He holds a BA in Art Education, an MA in Social Science (political theory and 20th-century U.S. history emphasis), and a PhD in Education (curriculum emphasis). Current research interests focus on the applicability of historical "classic" theories and the practice of democratic and ethical functioning at both the individual and system levels to current educational milieus. Recent publications include *Memories of Paulo* (Sense Publishers, 2010); "Liberation Pedagogy," in L. Sullivan (Ed.), *The Sage Glossary of the Social and Behavioral Sciences* (Sage, 2009); *La Escuela Freire: Academy for Culture, Leadership, and Civic Engagement* (2009; www.rus-ameeduu forum.com); and "Learning Moments: Raging a Bit, and with Hope," in S. Nieto (Ed.), *Dear Paulo: Letters from Those Who Dare Teach* (Paradigm, 2008).

Index

CRITICAL EDUCATION & ETHICS

Barry Kanpol
General Editor

The Critical Education and Ethics series intends to systematically analyze the pitfalls of social structures such as race, class, and gender as they relate to educational issues. Books in the series contain theoretical work grounded in pragmatic, society-changing practices. The series places value on ethical responses, as prophetic commitments to change the conditions under which education takes place.

The series aims to (1) Further the ethical understanding linking broader social issues to education by exploring the environmental, health-related, and faith/spiritual responses to our educational times and policy, and (2) Ground these works in the everyday world of the classroom, viewing how schools are impacted by what critical researchers do. Both theoretically and practically, the series aims to identify itself as an agent for community change.

The Critical Education and Ethics series welcomes work from emerging scholars as well as those already established in the field.

For additional information about this series or for the submission of manuscripts, please contact Dr. Kanpol (Indiana University—Purdue University Fort Wayne) at kanpolb@ipfw.edu.